Timely Questions
Timeless Wisdom

In conversation at Kellogg College,
University of Oxford

Ringu Tulku Rinpoche

with Mary Heneghan

Published in the Tibetan Year of the Wood Dragon, February 2025
by *Ocean of Wisdom* Publishing

Ocean of Wisdom Publishing is a non-profit organisation, under the
umbrella of Bodhicharya, registered as a Community Interest Company
at Hill House, Old Road, Shotover Hill, Oxford, OX3 8TA, United Kingdom

Creative Commons © 2025
This work is openly licensed under Creative Commons Licence
CC BY-NC-SA 4.0 (see end of book for details)

Ringu Tulku asserts the moral right to be identified as the author of this work

Compiled and edited by Mary Heneghan

ISBN 978-1-0686400-1-8

Teaching sources:

In conversation with Ringu Tulku Rinpoche at Kellogg College, University of Oxford.
June 2023

'Sangha, the third jewel' hosted by White Tara Group at Thrangu House,
Oxford. May 2024

'Joy and rejoicing' hosted by Ela Crain in Sintra, Portugal. August 2024

'Approaching Mahamudra' and end of teaching tour talk, Bodhicharya Berlin.
October 2024

'The Eightfold Path' Humkara Dzong, Portugal. August 2010

Typesetting & Design: Spiffing Publishing & *Ocean of Wisdom* Publishing

Cover image: Radcliffe Camera, Bodleian Library, University of Oxford

Back cover image: Ringu Tulku at the Botanical Gardens, University of Oxford.
Ringu Tulku teaching at Friends Meeting House, Oxford; taken by Peter Budd

Timely Questions
Timeless Wisdom

Ocean *of* **Wisdom**
PUBLISHING

Bodhicharya
AWAKEN THE HEART BY OPENING THE MIND

Kellogg College
University of Oxford

Contents

Foreword 1
Preface 5
Introduction 7

In Conversation at Kellogg College

Living and working in harmony 11
Education 14
Leadership 16
Wisdom 17
What dies and what doesn't die? 23
Facing the ecological crisis 25
Learning over time 29

It is a Pleasure to be a Student 33

Living Well

Awaken the heart by opening the mind 35
Changing our attitude to change our life 37
Joy and rejoicing 41
Not getting triggered 43
Direction in life 44
Karma and creating a path 47
Foundational understanding 51
Three sacred principles 53

Walking a Noble Path
- Four Noble Truths 55
- Causes of suffering 56
- The Eightfold Path and Right View 58
- Humility 62
- Right Thought 64
- Change and continuity 68
- Love and attachment 71
- Right Speech 74
- Good communication 75
- Time and space 78

Dedication 87

Glossary 89

Acknowledgements 95

About the Author 97

Foreword

It was a genuine pleasure to welcome Ringu Tulku as our guest at Kellogg College. It is now a great honour to have been invited to contribute the Foreword to this short book, based on the talk delivered by Ringu Tulku, and the subsequent discussion during his visit.

It is fitting that both Ringu Tulku and Kellogg College began learning journeys at the same time, in 1990. That is the year Ringu Tulku embarked on his international travels to teach and listen and learn, to make friends and contacts, and to enhance his experience and wisdom – from which we benefited during his visit.

This was also the year that the University of Oxford decided that, for the first time, people from across the world could study for a postgraduate degree without having to be resident in Oxford. Students would be permitted, also for the first time, to continue with paid work whilst studying for an Oxford degree. This was the start of flexible and distance learning for Oxford degrees. And our college was established to support these students.

During Ringu Tulku's visit to Kellogg College it became clear that we had derived similar lessons and conclusions from our respective learning journeys, on which we had both embarked in 1990. Both Ringu Tulku and Kellogg College had come to appreciate the value of lifelong learning, of social and environmental sustainability, and of internationalism. These are values which Ringu Tulku and Kellogg College are committed to promoting, practising, and achieving on local and global scales.

There are currently strong head winds against such progress. But this makes our joint endeavours all the more important, rather than any less so. That is the spirit in which this book is published, as a contribution to our collective efforts to promote lifelong learning, social and environmental sustainability, and internationalism. Thank you, Ringu Tulku!

Professor Jonathan Michie OBE FAcSS
President, Kellogg College
University of Oxford

Left to right: Professor Jonathan Michie, President of Kellogg College; Ringu Tulku Rinpoche; Sonam Tsering Frasi, Northern European representative for His Holiness the Dalai Lama; Mary Heneghan

Preface

In the summer of 2023, Ringu Tulku was invited to give a Question-and-Answer talk at Kellogg College, part of the University of Oxford. Ringu Tulku first came to the West around the start of 1990, from his home in Sikkim, Northern India, at the request of fellow Tibetan lineage-holders, then already living in the U.K. This marked the start of his teaching in the West, since which he has been invited to talk at innumerable conferences, Buddhist centres, universities, institutions and monasteries, as well as meeting with many smaller and more personal groups. His popularity now means his teaching tours take up much of his year and in 2024, for example, he taught at 55 centres in 22 countries over a period of six months.

Ringu Tulku holds a vast store of the academic and traditional lineage teachings of Buddhism, as they were preserved in Tibet, from their origins in India. He also holds a genuine interest to meet and connect with people from all over the world. He once described himself as 'always a student,' maintaining an interest to learn and discuss with all the many people he has been meeting, an interest we now benefit from in his teachings.

Kellogg College is one of the more newly-established colleges of Oxford University, founded in 1990 for graduate study. It has particularly pioneered and specialised in lifelong learning, supporting many degrees in part-time and distance-learning formats, in all fields of the humanities, medicine, and the natural and social sciences. Kellogg is also dedicated to international inclusivity, with students and fellows coming from an enormously wide range of locations, ethnicities and backgrounds from around the world, creating the truly international fabric of the college. Always keen to foster international exchange and learning, Kellogg has hosted many prominent speakers over the years, such as Archbishop Desmond Tutu, His Royal Highness King Charles (when he was Prince Charles), and Ban Ki-moon.

As part of these endeavours, the college organises an ongoing series of 'In conversation with …' events. This was the format in which Ringu Tulku was invited to the college in June 2023. The conversation held then forms the basis of this small book, with further material added from questions asked later, and from Ringu Tulku's extensive body of teachings given over the years, to supplement the discussion and expand on topics raised during the conversation.

The topics covered include: living and working together in harmony; leadership, education and learning; the nature of wisdom and knowledge; and how to approach day to day issues, as well as crises, of our time. The text leads into some of Ringu Tulku's more general Buddhist teachings, expanding and deepening themes such as the importance of our attitude, karma and creating a path in life. It finishes by introducing the Eightfold Path, which Buddha taught as a means of freeing ourselves from confusion and suffering.

We hope you enjoy this conversation with Ringu Tulku, and the timeless wisdom it offers for the questions of our times.

Introduction

Ringu Tulku Rinpoche may be introduced as a high lama, or teacher, from the Tibetan Kagyu lineage of Buddhist teaching. All Buddhism originated in India but then teachings were brought to Tibet many centuries ago and maintained through a number of lineages. The Kagyu lineage, one of these, is sometimes called the 'Lineage of Meaning and Blessing' or the 'Oral Lineage,' alluding to the importance of person-to-person transmission of Buddha's original teachings and practitioners' realisation.

The forefathers of the Kagyu lineage date back to the 11th Century, starting with Tilopa, an Indian spiritual adept who lived around 988 – 1069 AD. The transmission of this lineage can be traced, master to disciple, from then to the present day, through the first Karmapa (the head of the Karma Kagyu lineage, Dusum Khyenpa) 900 years ago, to His Holiness the 17th Karmapa, Ogyen Trinley Dorje. His Holiness explains the importance of lineage in this context: "As a lineage guru [Dusum Khyenpa] is the wellspring of a long and unbroken series of masters and disciples who passed the Karma Kagyu lineage from one to the other in what we call the Golden Rosary. All the goodness that these masters created in the world over the past 900 years can be traced to the original kindness of Dusum Khyenpa."

As I was preparing for this conversation with Ringu Tulku at Kellogg College, I was contemplating these timelines of learning and study and of holding teachings. It occurred to me that here, in Oxford, a similarly long line of continuous teaching and study was being established over a comparable time period. There is no exact start date for the University of Oxford, but there is evidence of teaching in Oxford from the 11th Century (1096) onwards. The first colleges were established in 1249 and some of the earliest academic halls were maintained by monastic orders, as monastic colleges began to replace monasteries as centres of theological study. Early monastic influence at Oxford University can also be seen through the patron saint of Oxford, Saint Frideswide, who was abbess of a nunnery in Oxford in the 8th Century, which later provided the central element around which Christ Church College was founded.

In these ways, both Oxford University and the Tibetan Karma Kagyu lineage have a history of around 900 years of continuous existence. Ringu Tulku himself has trained extensively with many great masters of this lineage, and of the other major lineages of Tibetan Buddhism, including His Holiness the 16th Karmapa and His Holiness Dilgo Khyentse Rinpoche. And, although Ringu Tulku prefaced his first answer in the conversation at Kellogg College by explaining that he is not a high lama at all – "just someone who is invited to speak in many places because I speak English well" - I am certain that those who read the teachings shared within this book will differ with that view.

Ringu Tulku was originally taught English, incidentally, by a remarkable, Oxford-educated, woman called Freda Bedi. Freda married an Indian scholar she met while they were both studying at Oxford and she and her husband assisted Mahatma Gandhi closely in his efforts. Later, Freda founded the Young Lama's Home School in Dalhousie, India, where Tibetan tulkus and lamas, newly in India as refugees from their homeland, could learn and develop their traditional studies, as well as learning English and a basic Western education. Ringu Tulku was the youngest boy at the Young Lama's Home School, at around ten years old, and he sometimes travelled with Freda; one year she promised him she would teach him English as her Christmas present to him. Thank goodness, I think, for this network of connections which has brought us to this point.

Ringu Tulku introduces us here, in simple terms, to profound Buddhist wisdom and insights. These include the importance of kindness and tolerance in addressing both personal and social challenges. He shares teachings about how we and all things exist, in an interdependent flow of openness, ever-changing and 'unpindownable,' and not as fixed as we usually assume. This is key to understanding human conflict and suffering, and thus the gradual freedom that can arise as we come to properly understand our own hearts and minds. As such, the teachings in this book offer an introduction to the timeless wisdom of Buddhism, as well as a resource for those wishing to understand more deeply the ways in which our minds can be a source of healing, both for ourselves and our world.

We hope you find this presentation helpful.

Mary Heneghan
for *Ocean of Wisdom* Publishing

In Conversation at Kellogg College

Living and working in harmony

MH: We were having some discussions here in Oxford, amongst friends and colleagues, in order to put together some questions to ask on this occasion, which everyone might be interested in, and this first one came out of a conversation with my husband, Carl. We were talking about the state of the world: all the conflicts and wars; people being displaced as a result of these conflicts, or due to persecution of many types; there are so many distressing instances of these, these days.

Then we got to talking about the way we all now use the internet and social media; how they facilitate so much, but at the same time they can also breed feelings of separation, alienation, and adversarial or combative attitudes, even generating 'hate campaigns' in the extreme. We've also just come through the years of Covid pandemic and its repercussions, where everyone experienced some degree of enforced isolation, which seems to have led in some instances to misunderstanding, polarisation and fragmentation, through some kind of disconnection.

So, the question we wanted to ask was: In the context of these realities of life, what can the Buddhist teachings offer, in terms of guidance on how to live and work in harmony with each other?

RTR: Of course, harmony is very important, as you all know. If there is no harmony, then nothing works. If the elements in our body are not in harmony, we become sick. And when they become less and less in harmony, we could even die. It is the same case for everything: whether it's a society, a family, our own emotions, or how we deal with others and how we work together. If there is no harmony, then it doesn't work. Because everything works with many different elements together. There is nothing that is only one thing. And nothing that works if only one part works; every part has to work. Every part has to work in a good way, in a healthy way. So, therefore, harmony is essential in every field and every situation.

How to bring that harmony is, of course, not always easy. Over my lifetime, I have often been involved in inter-religious dialogues and things like that. Once I was in Varanasi; I was just roaming around a big stupa at Sarnath, one of the important Buddhist places, and someone there came up to me and was trying to challenge me a little bit. He was saying, "Oh, you religious people are so bad. There are so many religions and you are always fighting amongst yourselves. If there was just one religion, it would be so much better."

I also wanted to debate with this person, myself – in fact, this is something that is traditionally very much used in Tibetan Buddhism, we use debating a lot to try and learn through debate. Not just to defeat each other, but mainly to explore different ideas; to share our reasoning with each other and investigate from different points of view. But gradually through my life, I have learned, in a hard way, that you cannot really convince anybody just through debating.

People have to want to understand and to learn. Then, if people really want to learn, then you can talk with them and may convince them of something. But unless this is the case, however good your logic is, you will not be able to convince anyone. I had to learn this the hard way.

So anyhow, I replied to this man at Sarnath, "It is not necessarily so, that if there was only one religion there would be harmony, because there could be 'this school' and 'that school' or 'this section' and 'that section.' Even if you have one college, you have different departments or sections. Even in one family, you can have a 'father's side' and a 'mother's side' and things like that. And even if there is no organisation, we always experience things as 'I' and 'other.' And as soon as there is two, you can have conflict.

The main thing is whether different sides want to work together - with some understanding of each other, and with a certain humility and sense of respect towards each other. Only that can lead to harmony, and if that harmony is there, then even if there are lots of different things, it doesn't really matter. There is always difference of opinions. You can't have only one view or only one type of view, and in fact it's not good if there is only one way of looking at things. There are always many different views, different ways and different methods and different interests. People are not always the same so, therefore, different things can be very useful. The only thing is that we need to accept that; we need to know and understand that these different things are okay because these different views and different methods are for suiting and working for different people. If I understand how this is a good thing, then I can accept and respect it. Then there will be harmony.

So, therefore, I think harmony is respecting each other and understanding each other. And then having an open mind to be able to accommodate, and have some kind of tolerance of, differences. If that is there, then there can be harmony. And of course, this kind of harmony is a very big subject and I think it is the most important thing, because if there is no harmony then nothing works, whether it is a society, your own body, or even your mind. If you don't have harmony in your mind, you become unhealthy.

That is the main understanding and I think it is also what Buddhism tries to teach, to bring harmony in many different things. Buddha always said that there are many different paths and that is not bad, it is good, because people are not all the same so they need different approaches, different paths, different methods. So, there is nothing wrong with many views. It is not that I have to follow and practise all of them. Those that are suitable for me, I can follow. And those that are not suitable for me but are suitable for someone else, I should not only accept that but I can also respect it, and help to preserve and maintain that. This is the understanding from a Buddhist point of view.

Education

MH: There was a tweet from His Holiness the Dalai Lama's office recently that I wonder if it fits in with what you've just shared:

"Education should include training in how to be calm and unafraid. Since scientists now recognise the significance of warm-heartedness and peace of mind in personal and social well-being, it's time training to cultivate such qualities was included in the general education system."

Do you think that might be part of the fostering of this harmony you are talking about, Rinpoche? Do you have any further thoughts on that?

RTR: Yes, of course, education is to try to develop our wisdom, from the Buddhist point of view, meaning trying to understand the information and details about things and also the nature of things. It is important to have knowledge and wisdom. Knowledge is knowing the details of things: how things are, how things are made, what are the causes and conditions of things, all the different details about things. But wisdom is regarded as more important because wisdom is about having an idea, an understanding and the experience of how to solve problems. Whatever situation you are in, wisdom is knowing how to deal with that situation: What is the best way to solve a problem or resolve a whole situation in the most positive way, and so resolve all the causes and conditions of your problems. To have that understanding is wisdom.

Wisdom comes not only through having knowledge, but requires a deeper understanding of how people's emotions work and your own possibilities in dealing with situations. When you have a little bit of experience of that, then you become more ready to deal with and face anything in the world, any situation. You can learn different things, that is relatively easy, that is acquiring information. But to have the capacity to be okay in any situation, that takes wisdom, which is a different kind of learning. There is a saying, "The best kind of education means that if you have to be a servant, you are able to serve hundreds of people in the right way; if you have to become a leader, then you are able to lead thousands of people in the right way. If you become like that, then you are educated." Because when you have that kind of understanding or inner wisdom then you are able to deal with situations and people and relationships, but you are also able to deal with your own emotions and state of mind and deeper aspects.

When these two, knowledge and wisdom, are developed together, then it is education. So, education, from a Buddhist point of view, is seen as learning *about* things but also learning about the *nature* of things: about yourself and how to deal with things within your experience. These two together become education from a Buddhist point of view. So, once you reach a certain level of education, you don't have to be so afraid, you can be more kind and compassionate and wiser. When that happens, it's a true education, I think.

Leadership

MH: I don't know if there's anything more to be said here, Rinpoche, about the aspect of being a good leader? It was something I was talking to Jonathan about, the President of Kellogg College. The way in which Kellogg College is a graduate college means that many of the students here might already be in positions of leadership in different ways. And of course, it may fall to any of us to lead, in small ways or big ways, at different times.

Based on your own experiences and all the many and various leaders and people you have met, what advice would you give to someone taking on some form of leadership? How does one lead most effectively?

RTR: Of course, there are many things to say about this, but I have always found that people who are really good leaders are interested in people and what those people think and what they want. A good leader is not somebody who imposes their ideas on others but who really wants to learn and become one of them, not just being remote and 'up there' giving orders, but really working together. I have found those who really work together with others and who can bring people together and inspire them to work together in a harmonious way, they are really good leaders.

Wisdom

MH: I wonder, also, if there's anything more you could say about that aspect of wisdom you were talking about? The Buddhist teachings are very much concerned with developing compassion and wisdom, and this wisdom is talked about in different ways and at different levels. Sometimes it might be talked about at the relative level, which I guess is what you were talking about in terms of having the wisdom to know how to meet situations and deal with our lives. And then there's also a more ultimate or absolute level in which wisdom is talked about in the Buddhist teachings. I wanted to ask how such an understanding, of how things really exist, in a way, can inform our lives, perhaps again in terms of living more harmoniously? How does the relationship between the two work? How can this deeper understanding feed into our lives?

RTR: From the Buddhist point of view, we talk about two levels of wisdom. One is 'worldly wisdom' and another is sometimes called 'transcendental wisdom.' Worldly wisdom includes different kinds of knowledge, about health, about science, about how to understand and run things, how to work in a society, things like that. All these usually come under the umbrella of worldly wisdom; this also includes how we have to be considerate, kind and compassionate towards each other, and so forth - whatever is required so that society, individuals and relationships can all function in a good way, in a positive way. This kind of wisdom could all be called worldly wisdom.

Then, transcendental wisdom, from the Buddhist point of view, is also very important. If you want to look into the deeper causes of all our suffering and problems in life, then you find it is mainly due to our negative emotions and states of mind. These include anger and hatred, a whole group of that kind of emotions. Then, too much greed, attachment and craving, that kind of group of emotions. Too much envy and jealousy, those kinds of emotions or states. Too much arrogance and negative pride, that group. And then ignorance, or not understanding clearly and misunderstanding, those kinds of mind states. These five are the main groups of negative states of mind and are regarded as the main causes of all our suffering and problems, both as individuals, within ourselves, and throughout society.

For example, we have wars. If you look into the history of humankind, almost all the way through, it is a history of wars. When there are wars, everybody suffers. People kill each other; people torture each other and bring all kinds of suffering and pain to each other. Why do we have wars? If we look into it a little bit deeply, we can understand, without any doubt, that these wars happen because of our hatred and anger, because of greed, because of jealousy, because of arrogance, and because of misunderstanding. All of these are what lead to wars. And not only wars on national and international levels, but any kind of conflict. For example, within a family. Or even within ourselves, individually: all kinds of disturbances within our mind or within ourself are caused by these negative mind states.

So, from the Buddhist point of view, unless we find a way to deal with these and transform them, we cannot find lasting peace, or lasting happiness, or lasting solutions to our pain and problems. So that is why, when we talk about practising dharma or following the Buddhist teachings in a very deep way, in order to become enlightened and so forth, that is what we are talking about: deeply and completely uprooting these causes of suffering. And for that, the main antidotes or opposites states of mind, are two: one is compassion and the other is wisdom. And here, wisdom means this transcendental wisdom.

What is the opposite of anger and hatred? Compassion and kindness. The opposite of too much greed and craving is also compassion and kindness. The opposite of too much jealousy and envy is kindness and compassion. The opposite of too much pride and arrogance is kindness and compassion. So, real, genuine kindness and compassion are very important as the solution to many problems. If we could all be kind to each other, many problems would be solved simply by that.

Sometimes we feel that this is not possible. How can all the people be kind and compassionate to each other? But if we look a little bit deeply we see that there is no one who does not want to be treated with kindness and compassion. And not only that, but we find that, when we can be kind and compassionate ourselves, we feel good. When we feel anger and hatred and all the negative states of mind we experience, we feel disturbed. When we feel kind and compassionate, we feel joyful and happy and satisfied. So, if all of us are like that, why is this so difficult? How come we are not all kind and compassionate to each other? The main reason is because of ignorance. Firstly, we don't even dare to believe that this is possible. Even though we know it would be something very good, we do not dare to even feel that it is something that could be possible. Because if this were possible, there would be no more wars, there would be no more atrocities, there would be no more conflicts, immediately, from this day, if everybody started to behave in that way. This is how important this is.

So, compassion becomes a very important thing in Buddhism, and for everybody generally. I don't think there is any religion or spiritual path or code of morality which does not teach compassion and loving-kindness. It is one of the most important things, generally, as well as from the Buddhist point of view. But, in order to bring about real, complete compassion, and uproot our negative emotions and negative states of mind, the worldly kind of compassion alone is not enough. It can reduce these negative emotions but unless we develop this transcendental wisdom we are talking about we cannot totally uproot them. That is the Buddhist way of seeing things.

As long as we have this view that 'I am' – that I exist, that I am like 'this,' and others are 'there' and like 'that' - it affects our whole experience. This is 'me' and 'mine,' those are 'others' and 'theirs.' When I have this kind of notion, very strongly, then whatever I see there as 'other' I start to think 'that is very nice, I want it' or 'that is not very nice, I don't want it' and I react with attachment or with aversion. If there is something nice, I want to get it, so I run after it. If there is something not nice, I want to get rid of it so I try to run away from it. As long as that way of action and reaction is there, then all these emotions come up. Anger, hatred and all these kinds of difficult emotions come up. If I am to eliminate this way of relating to myself and others, then I need to understand deeply how I am, how I exist and how everything exists. And that is not necessarily easy. So, therefore, there are lots of teachings and reflections and meditations to help us investigate and try to understand the nature of things: the nature of phenomena and the nature of myself.

Within that, we try to understand interdependence and dependent-arising. To try to describe this in a very simple or quick way, we could say that everything that exists, everything we could think about, exists in a way which is not as one thing existing totally on its own. Everything is a totally dependently-existing thing, a relatively-existing thing. Nothing exists totally, truly, on its own. For instance, everything is changing. Nothing remains the same. Everything changes; and why does everything change? Because nothing is just one thing; everything is made of so many parts, so many causes and so many conditions. And all these conditions and causes and parts keep on changing.

This applies to me too, to each of us: are we the same one that we were born as? We think we are the same person as we were born as, but are we really the same one? I keep on changing. Even my mother wouldn't recognise me now if she saw me! Nothing remains the same; everything keeps on changing. For instance, one scientist told me that every cell in your body is replaced after every seven years, or nine years, or so. So, after every seven to nine years, there is not even one cell in your body which is the same. So, I have changed ten times over in my lifetime.

So, therefore, we have a situation of interdependence, as it is called from the Buddhist point of view. Interdependence is sometimes described in Buddhism as emptiness. If you look deeply there is nothing truly existing as one thing. Myself also. When I see myself, not as a 'me' that I strongly identify with, as one thing, I experience myself as a changing thing. I am like a process, like a river. You look at a river, and you think that is the same river that has always been there, perhaps for hundreds of years. But if you look deeply, the river is a flowing block of water. Even compared to five minutes ago, the river is not the same. The water that was there a minute ago is not there anymore. But we think it is the same water, the same river.

If we understand this deeply, then our self-centredness – that 'this is me' – can be deeply changed and we experience ourselves a bit differently. When we experience in this way, we see clearly that there is no point being upset: who is upset, and for what, hating what? It leads to a completely different experience. Through that kind of wisdom, we can have a totally different way of seeing ourselves and seeing phenomena. And that can totally uproot our habitual ways of looking at ourselves and others. It completely widens our way of looking at all phenomena. From that point of view, we can be completely kind and compassionate without holding on to any special individual thing, and then the ultimate kind of wisdom can arise. And that, from the Buddhist point of view, is called enlightenment or Buddhahood.

Even if we cannot totally accomplish that, at least if we can see how much things are changing, how dependent they are, how interdependent they are, that will make us a little more able to be less greedy and selfish, and more kind and compassionate. And that, in a deep way, might be able to solve the problems we have in the world, including, for example, the ecological problems we have. These also basically come from these kinds of causes, from our negative mind states.

So, these two levels of wisdom, both worldly and transcendental, encompass the Buddhist way of wisdom.

What dies and what doesn't die?

DF: You've already talked quite a bit about what I wanted to ask about: transcendental wisdom and our sense of our everyday self, the aspect of us that has thoughts and emotions and wants things and doesn't want things; and how the ignorance of overly identifying with that is the cause of a lot of our problems.

Yesterday we were saying prayers for a great master who has died recently, Thrangu Rinpoche, and I was thinking about how those prayers had two aspects. One was lamenting what had died, as in, "We miss you, we wish you were still with us." The other was asking for him to come back. So there seems to be two things there. I would call it the everyday self, which we miss, and the more transcendental self, which is perhaps greater than us.

I wanted to ask about the relationship between the two, but to some extent you've covered that. So, now I'm wondering what is it that dies and what is it that doesn't die? Is there any aspect of that kind of transcendental 'being' that is always there? It seems to me it's not just the body that dies, even for a great master such as Thrangu Rinpoche, but also who we feel they were in the world.

RTR: I think it's like this; everything changes. We can actually see that everything changes, everyone changes. Even very highly realised people, including Buddhas and Jesus and everybody, everyone dies and passes away. This is a fact and we need to understand that. When we die, change is obvious but we don't have to die to change. Even when we are not dying, when we are living, there is always changing. We don't have to die to change. We change all the time, in every moment, in our body. I don't know how many millions of cells are dying every day and how many are growing, but it's all a process of changing; and the process of changing is not only at the time of death, but all the time.

When we die, we call it a death, because it's something much more obvious and strong. Of course, when somebody dies who is kind and loving and greatly valued by us, we feel sad. We miss them. We don't want them to die; we want them to be with us. And also, when it comes to very positive beings, if there are more of them among us, it will be better for all of us. So, we pray that those positive beings, those great beings, live long and stay with us for a longer time. But if we look more deeply into it, and really understand from that ultimate wisdom point of view, we can see clearly that both birth and death, living and dying, happen in the same way. Death is relatively dying, but *truly* what is dying? If something does not exist completely in its own way, on its own, then you can't say that it dies. So, therefore, when we actually, very clearly, experientially perceive things as they are, then in a way, we are freed from death.

This wisdom is not something that is 'different,' something that we have to get. Wisdom is to understand the way things actually are. It's not that there is a different thing happening for different people, depending on the wisdom they have. The same thing is happening, but how we see things may be different. If we perceive things as they actually are, then we have wisdom. If we don't perceive things as they are, then we have ignorance. The person who can see this clearly, sees that 'death' is just another change, and that in fact there is no thing called death. This is why some people can face death without fear. But as long as we don't have that experience of wisdom, then we are afraid of death and we don't want to die; and when somebody dies, we feel very sad and all our suffering and problems around that come up.

That's why this ultimate kind of wisdom becomes very important because, with that, then you truly understand very deeply how things are. And at that time, maybe there is nothing called death. But until then, there is death and we have all the problems that we have.

Facing the ecological crisis

FDC: My question is about the ecological emergency we are facing, which you touched on earlier. In 2021, the UN General Secretary, Antonio Guterres, summarised the Inter-Governmental Report on Climate Change as 'code red for humanity.' And not only human beings, but many other life forms, are now threatened by climate change. How do you respond to this existential threat as a Buddhist?

RTR: Buddhists always talk about impermanence. We try to actually meditate on impermanence and understand deeply about impermanence. And it is felt that, if we could really understand impermanence very deeply, we wouldn't become so greedy. We would be able to be a little bit more contented. We would be able to live without wanting more and more and more and, instead, we could enjoy more and more and more about what we have. This is contentment.

I am told by the scientists themselves that the ecological problems we face are basically happening because of over-exploiting our Earth and our natural resources. And because of modern technology we can do this much more effectively, to the extent that now we are on the verge of destroying our home. The relationship between ourselves and our Earth, we together with all other animals, is the relationship of container and contained. The Earth is the container and we are the contained. And if there is no container, we cannot have the contained. Just as how, if I break this glass, the water in it will no longer be there, it will spill out. So, if we understand that deeply, that might change how we do things.

Now they say we are almost too late. And this brings another problem. I have been attending conferences on climate change and environmental issues, and scientists have been presenting all the evidence and data at these. Many people can get very depressed, with a real sense of hopelessness. And some people are feeling that, if there is nothing that can be done and if it brings a sense of hopelessness, what is the use in having a conference for that? So, they asked me to say something which might offer some encouragement or a positive side to it all. I didn't know what to say, but recently I read something by one of the scientists at Oxford University which I found interesting. He said he used to think the climate crisis was a scientific problem that was the job of the scientists to address, but then he found that it is not something to be solved by scientists alone, because it involves all the human beings. So, everybody has to be involved, and especially the spiritual and religious people.

Everybody has to be involved, this is true. But it is very difficult to go back. There are lots of developed countries whose economic development comes from exploitation of resources. And those countries that are not so developed do not want to stop developing because of what the other countries have done to create this situation. So, I was wondering how it would be possible to do something about all this. And what I thought was: Yes, it is a problem. This is something we have to recognise; we need to understand and we need to do something, but sometimes I see that people are too shocked, too angry and too upset by the information so that they feel hopeless. I have even heard young people say that they don't even want to do anything or live any more, because there is no future. Such hopelessness does not help to change anything.

I think it cannot be hopeless. I think there could be some solution. Because everything is interdependent. Interdependent means everything is like it is, including our environment, because of many causes and conditions. So, therefore, in this interdependent situation, if you can take one thing out, even a seemingly-small thing, it could change everything - because it is interdependent. Or similarly, if you put one thing in that is not there already, it could also change everything. This happens. This has happened many different times in many different ways. Many things that we thought were not possible to change, changed very quickly, because some element came in and had a strong effect. So, this could happen in this case.

I don't know if it is true, but it seems to me that this problem was mainly created by science and technology. If those methods of advancement were not there, we would not have had such an impact on the Earth so quickly. Now I think it is the scientists who have to fix it, and I think they can. They have to find something that would change the process, in a very intelligent way. If they can produce so many miraculous things, why can't they also produce some solution to this problem? It's just that the most brilliant minds have to be focussed on it. I think it is not impossible.

And at the same time, we need to change our own way of living, so that it is not based on greed and wanting more and more. Rather, we can learn to live more harmoniously and contentedly and kindly towards each other so that we can work together. If we can become more like that, then most probably things can change. It is not impossible that things can change.

There are also many predictions made within the Buddhist teachings. Some talk about 'five degenerations,' and things like that, which predict and describe how things are currently degenerating. Mainly things are degenerating because of our way of seeing. Our negative emotions have become too raw and too strong. Our self-centredness takes over and then we lose our moral codes of living, and this leads to stronger and more prevalent negative states of mind. But the predictions say that if we really worked on our compassion, or Bodhicitta [the awakened heart-mind of wisdom and compassion], this situation could change. It is said that there can be many loops within the degenerative times, and there can still be what is called a 'golden age,' and that these golden ages can be created by us in that way. It is not about the time, or the era, but about us and our attitudes. If we really want this to come about, and really try and work towards that, there can be a golden age any time. This is the main idea from the Buddhist point of view.

MH: That is really lovely to hear.

Learning over time

JM: I liked the point about 900 years of the Kagyu lineage and 900 years of Oxford University. I should explain, though, this college isn't 900 years old – but we will be! I know also that you started your teaching and traveling in the West around 1990, just over 30 years ago, which is also when Kellogg College was actually founded. I think we've learnt some things, since then, about how we can best learn and teach.

Kellogg is the most diverse college in the University, and the most international and inter-disciplinary college, because we believe in learning from people from other countries and cultures, other disciplines and backgrounds, other mindsets. In that vein, everything you've shared with us already has been really helpful and I wonder if there's anything else you've learnt during your traveling and learning and teaching over the past 33 years that might be relevant to us in that way?

RTR: I wonder what I have learnt over the past 33 years, or even over the past 70 years! I have learnt that I have a lot more to learn. This is something that is very clear to me, because you can never learn enough. Every day and every time you meet somebody and everywhere you go, you learn something new. It's not something you can count. But I think life is about learning. You never stop learning. I think that's one important lesson that I've learnt. You can never be anything but a student all the time. When you stop learning, then you finish your life. I see it like that. I have learnt a lot and I am still hoping to learn more. This event itself is a learning process and I have been very happy to meet everyone here and come to this wonderful place.

When I first travelled out of India, I came to England first, and then many other different countries. At first, compared to India and Nepal, which were the only places I had been in until then, I thought it was like heaven here. There didn't seem to be any of the problems we usually had. I thought everybody must be so extremely happy. Soon, however, I found out it's not exactly like that. I found that people here are not that happy, not that satisfied, and I came to understand that how happy you are is not to do with your life situation. It is to do with yourself. That was a very important learning for me.

The first time I came to this country, I met a professor who said to me he was going to commit suicide. I was surprised and asked why. He said his university – it was not Oxford! – had been going to send him to a conference in America but then they didn't send him, and then again that year they didn't either. So he was really upset and unhappy. I didn't know what to say so I said, "Well America must be a very lovely place to go, but is it worth dying for? Why don't you just go there anyway if you want to go there? Do you not have the money?" He said he had lots of money; it wasn't that.

This kind of thing totally shocked me. But it is a little bit like that. How you are, how happy you are, how satisfied you are, is totally dependent on your way of being and your way of seeing, how you perceive things. I have learned that.

I am very happy that I could travel to different countries and have the opportunity to learn many things. When I first came to the West, I thought the whole of the West was the same. Then slowly I learned about all the different countries and different languages and so forth. I still thought it was all mainly the same, the way people thought and so on, just with different languages and those kind of things. Slowly, slowly, though, I have found that it is not all the same at all.

I find this all very interesting. That's why, even though I am 70 now, I am still travelling all over the world and always meeting people. That is what I enjoy, meeting lots of people and learning from them.

It is a Pleasure to be a Student

I am a student.
I have been a student as long as I remember
And it is a pleasure to be a student.

It is a pleasure to learn that I don't know.
It is a pleasure to learn that I already know.
It is a pleasure to learn that I was mistaken.

It is a joy to learn from Great Masters.
It is a joy to learn by sharing what I learnt.
It is a joy to learn how to be what I am.

I seek to learn about the world around me.
I seek to learn about what I actually am.
I seek to learn how to be a proper human being.

Clouds show me the nature of my world.
Rivers show me the nature of myself.
Babies show me how to be more human.

I am a student.
I will be a student as long as I live.
And it is a pleasure to be a student.

Ringu Tulku
Gangtok, Sikkim, India. 2003

Living Well

Awaken the heart by opening the mind

MH: I wanted to ask about the organisation you set up, under the name of Bodhicharya, which refers to 'enlightened activities,' actions based on compassion and wisdom, and which has the banner 'Awaken the heart by opening the mind.' I remember this line catching my attention when I first came across the organisation, and I wondered if you could say something about why you chose this line: how opening the mind awakens the heart and what opening the mind refers to?

RTR: The heart and mind are very connected; this was my thinking with that phrase. If we are to open our hearts, and become more kind and compassionate and positive, we need to learn why it is so important. If we don't know why we should be kind to each other, then we won't become kind to each other. But if we see that we want everybody to be kind to us; and if somebody is kind to me, I feel very happy; and then we see that I am not the only one who feels like this – there is almost nobody who doesn't feel good when somebody is kind to them – then we can understand that everybody wants others to be kind to them.

If I can really understand this deeply, then at least I would try to remind myself to be kind to others. I would feel happy and joyful any time I was kind and I would know it wasn't the right way any time I was unkind. That understanding can slowly help us to transform ourselves, to open our hearts. Any transformation of our experience and personality has to be based on some kind of understanding. Intellectual understanding alone is not enough, but it is where things can start from.

YP: I can see from my own experience that, if I'm at peace in my own mind, then I am naturally kind. It's when fear is there, when my nervous system is in 'fight or flight' mode, that I become defensive. I'm not aware of ever really wanting to harm anyone or deliberately be unkind, but I am aware I can be defensive when I'm frightened. I think that understanding can be really helpful - how we're naturally kind when we're at ease, that it's naturally inherent in us, and how that never really leaves us. I don't think I realised, for a long time, how connected kindness is to a lack of fear.

RTR: That's right, it's very true. Fear, or doubt, suspicion and paranoia; feeling anxious about what is going to happen or how somebody is thinking about us; these all make us defensive, frightened, reactive and closed. It is very much like that.

Sometimes I think it is very important to understand that, yes, I am the way I am, I am not perfect; I have some positive qualities and some negative qualities. But regardless, people can project anything they want onto me. It is not the case that the way I am will be seen in the same way by everybody. If somebody is in a difficult, frightened or closed state of mind, he or she would also project that onto me. Whatever I am like, it is not the case that everybody would necessarily like me or be kind and understanding.

When I really understand that, I have no choice but to accept it. I see that there is no use always trying to work out what others are thinking about me. It's totally useless. We are samsaric beings; sometimes we see people in a very positive way, and sometimes others may not see us like that. I cannot control how others see me or react to me. If I say something, one person can understand it in one way and another can understand it in another way. So, I think it's very important not to worry too much about these things.

Changing our attitude to change our life

Everything changes. If we can understand this and remind ourselves of it when things are at their worst, I think it gives us the courage not to lose hope. And I think this is very important in life. Because it so often happens that when something negative happens, we think that that is the end and we give up.

Because I am a Buddhist teacher, people often ask me about meditation. Meditation is very good. It is very important. But in my own experience, meditation does not bring quick results. You have to learn meditation - and then you have to *do* it. The results can be very deep and very far-reaching but it takes time to bring such results through meditation. To change our attitude, on the other hand, can bring benefit almost immediately. We can always learn new ways of thinking and reacting. So therefore, I think it is very important to learn how to look at situations and remind ourselves of what is the right way, or best way, to approach them. In my life, this has given me a lot of help to face situations and life and problems, by doing that. Because it can give you another perspective.

There is a saying in one of the important classics of Buddhist teachings, which His Holiness the Dalai Lama often quotes and he always says it has helped him a lot: "If you see that you can do something to change a situation, then there is no need to get upset, or angry or worried about it, because you can do that thing. If you see that there is absolutely no way you can change that situation, whatever is happening, even if it is very difficult, what is the use of getting angry, upset or worried?" I think this is a very important way of looking at things.

When something difficult happens and we react by getting very upset, angry or worried, we act and react completely from negative emotions and then we can do very stupid things. Instead, we could remind ourselves when something difficult happens, to ask, "Is there something I can do to make things better, or not?" Most of the time, there is something you can do, at least to make things slightly better. If that is the case, then instead of wasting time being upset, we can start to do something to make things better. Then we already feel optimistic – being optimistic does not mean we have to solve all the problems; if we know things can become even a little bit better, that is optimistic in itself.

Otherwise, when anything difficult happens you can feel you have too many problems and you don't know how to solve them, and you get very upset and sad and 'down' and lost. That is something that happens to all of us sometimes, as I have seen from my own experience. Everybody can have problems. Poor people have their own problems. Rich people have their own problems. Powerful people have their own problems. Famous people have their own problems. There is no one who does not have any problems. But everybody also has some good things, nice, wonderful things in their life. And to remind ourselves of that is important.

There is a story about this, about a person who had lots of problems. In short, he had problem number one, problem number two… up to problem number ten. He was very much oppressed by all these problems; he was always thinking of them and could not solve them, so much so that he was at breaking point. He had a friend who wanted to help him but he had so many problems that there was no way to solve them. Then his friend heard that a certain person had arrived from somewhere, who was supposed to be very good at solving problems and giving advice. So, he went to his friend who had all these problems and suggested he go and see him. The man refused, saying no one could help him with all his problems, they were so difficult. His friend insisted that at least he would not lose anything if he went. So, he was persuaded to go.

He went to see the person who had been recommended and found him just sitting in a room looking very normal. So, he explained all his problems; problem number one, problem number two… up to problem number ten. Then, instead of giving him some hints about how to solve these problems, the person simply said, "Can you see?"

"Yes," replied the man, "my eyes are very good. That's not my problem. I have all these other problems."

"Can you see different colours around my room?" the person asked.

"Yes, I can see colours. That is not my problem. I told you all about my problems. If you have anything to say about them, I will be happy. Otherwise, I will go away. My eyesight is not a problem."

"How many red things are in my room?" He asked.

The man became very upset and angry but he looked around and counted the red things. "There are maybe ten red things in your room. But that is nothing to do with my problem!"

"How many blue things are there in my room?"

"I am not going to count blue things! That is not my problem!"

"Okay. You counted the red things in my room and you found that there were ten of them. You don't know how many blue things there are in my room because you didn't count them. You know you have these ten problems, because you have been counting them all the time. Do you know how many positive and good things there are in your life?"

"Well, I'm sure I have some positive and good things in my life, but I have not counted them."

"That is the problem you have. You go back and count all the good things in your life and then come back tomorrow."

So, the man went home and started to count all the good things in his life. And he found that he had many good things in his life, many more than ten. And the next day he came back and said, "Actually it is true. I have lots of good things in my life, more than ten."

"Yes," said the man. "That is how it is. Everybody has problems in their life. And some of those problems might have solutions. Some might get solved more quickly, some might take time to solve. Some of them may never be solved. You may have to live with them. But you also have many good things in your life. And you need to remind yourself of those good things, and enjoy those good things. If you can enjoy those positive things you have in your life, you will immediately feel much better because you will be thinking of positive things.

"How we feel is not about how things are but where we focus our mind. So, if we focus on our positive things, we will be feeling positivity. It's not that we have to ignore our difficult things, we have to work on them, we have to try and solve them. But we also have to remind ourselves often of all the positive and good things. Focus your mind on that and enjoy those things and appreciate them. That will change your life." And it actually did. He stopped feeling so hopeless and lost.

So, how we focus our mind makes a big difference to our experience. There are always lots of problems but also lots of good things happening in our lives. If we can find balance and focus on all the good things, then we can always feel good, even when we have to tackle problems as well. That is something that is very useful in life, I think, because there is nobody that does not have problems.

Joy and rejoicing

Joy and rejoicing are also very important. Rejoicing in the good fortune and well-being of others is the opposite of jealousy and envy. In the Indian language this quality is called *mudita* and it is something that not many people talk about or think about. Even regarding compassion and kindness; almost everybody can feel compassion and kindness towards those who are suffering and have problems. Everybody would at least wish well to those people, and they may also try to help them. But if somebody is much better off than you, people usually find it much harder to have that kind of attitude towards them. They feel a little jealousy or envy rather than wishing well to them. But that does not make sense, because they still have their own problems. So, instead of feeling envious or jealous, if I can feel rejoicing, it is so much better.

If somebody does something good, I genuinely feel joyful and rejoice. If somebody gets something better than I have, or something special, I can really rejoice that they have that. Whatever positive things anybody has or is doing or achieving, that person is happy because of that; there is no reason why you should be unhappy. That would just be making myself unhappy for no reason. It would not get me anything. It just makes me unhappy.

For example, let's say my neighbour gets a very nice car. Maybe I don't make friends with him because I feel jealous. But if instead I were to rejoice about his new car, I am happier, he is happier and immediately we become friends. And maybe I might even get a lift in the new car!

When you can feel happy at somebody else's positive things, you can be happy without spending anything. You are just happy because somebody has achieved something or somebody has received something good. You can then be happy all the time. You appreciate them, you may become friends, and you become a very positive person.

This is something which is not understood by many people but it makes a real difference in life. You know – somebody has a very nice dress, or they look very beautiful, you can just feel good about it. By your feeling good about positive things, you don't lose anything, but you gain happiness yourself. You feel positive, the other person feels good and you make a good kind of a connection. And then you can always feel good because there is something good happening somewhere all the time.

Not getting triggered

Question: From a practical standpoint, when someone triggers you, what are the tools you use so you don't react to them or get triggered in that moment?

RTR: I think the best thing is not to dwell on what they say. Don't elaborate on it yourself, by thinking things like, "I am not treated well… I am not loved… I am neglected… I am rejected… I am criticised…" If you think like this, then you will feel worse and worse. There is a saying, I don't know who said it, but I agree with it: "Ordinary people take revenge. Intelligent people forgive. Wise people ignore."

I thought this was a very wise saying. Because people do what they do. Nobody can force somebody to like you or to be nice to you, to be kind to you or to do the right thing. You cannot force anybody. No matter how strongly you wish or ask them to do that, they may not do it. So, however much you wish for something, it might not work. How people act towards you is up to them. Of course, it's not nice if they are unkind and so on. But that is up to them. What you have to concentrate on is that you are not hurt too much. I think that is the most important thing.

How much I am hurt by something has a lot to do with my own way of seeing things. If you feel very strongly that they should not behave like that, you will feel worse. But if you see clearly that that is their way of behaving, but that you don't need to hold on to it, you don't need to keep it in your mind and feel so hurt; you can let it be. In that way, you can keep your own integrity. You can keep your own peace of mind. In the end, this is more important for us than what others do or don't do. If we can do that, we don't need to be hurt too much by the actions of others, whatever they do.

Direction in life

Question: If life keeps pushing you in one direction, but you want to go in another direction, how can you clear your mind to see what is the right direction for you to go in?

RTR: Basically, we have to think carefully, "What is the most important thing for me - in the near future but also in a more ultimate way?" Most of us would think, "I want to be happy, I want to be free of suffering." But we might also wish we could do something that we could be proud of, so that in the long term, when we look back when at the end of our life, we could say we did something we are proud of, something that helped people. If I can think along those lines, then I can become clearer as to what I should do.

I have had a long life, myself, and I have had lots of different experiences in the course of my life. And what I feel is that if we get too fixated on anything, "I *have* to do *that*," sometimes it doesn't work out. If you are too tightly focused on one particular thing, I think you can miss many other opportunities that might actually be better for you. So sometimes I prefer to allow my mind to be more open so that if other opportunities or chances arise, that I did not think of before, then I can see if they would be good for me or beneficial, and then I might take those chances. I often find things get much easier through having that attitude.

If I have already fixated on my own way, just one solution, then I have to get everything together to achieve that, and it's a big struggle to get each thing in place. And then, even if I get all those things in place, in the end it's often not that great after all. But if I allow my mind to be more open and then, when the chances come I take them, then sometimes opportunities come along that I did not even think of. It is true that in our life sometimes bad things happen, so bad that we never even imagined them. But it is also true that good things can happen, things we never even dreamed of. So, I think it is good to let things happen like that.

Question: Attachment is often talked about in Buddhism as creating a lot of suffering. But what about for people who have ambitions, who want to get good things done, do you have any advice about how to stay focussed on the task and overcome obstacles and achieve your aims without being too attached to things in the process?

RTR: That is exactly what I was just trying to explain. Lots of things happen in our lives and sometimes they can go very well and sometimes there can be obstacles. So, therefore, we need to understand it is like that. There are ups and downs. When there is an up, there will be a down. When there is a down, there will be an up. So, we need to understand that problems and obstacles happen but that everything changes. If you have this understanding of impermanence that I was talking about, then you don't get so hurt and you can be flexible, you can do something else, or do things in another way. And sometimes it could become better.

Nobody has a life with only ups in it. There are always ups and downs. Of course, you have to try to see what can be done to make things better, you have to use any skills you have and be clever; but you also have to be clear that there will be obstacles but that they will pass and things are never unrecoverable. There is a saying, "If you have lost your wealth, nothing is lost. If you have lost your health, something is lost. If you have lost your character, everything is lost." I think there is a lot of truth in this. So, we have to understand how things are, and how we are, and keep our mind balanced. Because, even if you experience a setback in business or in your work, you still have your life, you still have your health, you still have many good things. We need to count the good things in our lives.

We can never see the whole picture; there are always many factors and many causes and conditions coming together in many ways, and how things will turn out is unknown. There is a story about an African king who had a minister who had a habit of saying, whatever happened, that it was the best thing that could have happened. One day the king was hunting and he had an accident and lost his finger. The whole country came to console him. But his advisor came and said, "Oh, maybe that is the best thing that could have happened." The king was so angry at this that he threw him into a dungeon.

A while later, the king was again hunting, when he was captured by cannibals. They were cleaning him, making him ready to be eaten, but when they found he had a finger missing, they released him because they couldn't eat him if he wasn't fully intact. The king was so relieved and remembered the advisor's words with remorse. So, he rushed to see the advisor in the dungeon and release him and apologise to him.

The advisor said, however, "Well, maybe it was the best thing that could have happened." The king again became angry, wondering why he would say such a thing. But the advisor explained, "Well, what I mean is, I usually go everywhere with you when I am advising you. I travel with you and probably I would have been hunting with you that day. I would not have left your side. So maybe I would have been caught by the cannibals also, and then I would have been eaten."

Question: Once we count the good things in our life, what about if there are many good opportunities coming up? Sometimes our path in life is clear, but sometimes there are multiple options, so how can we decide which ones to follow?

RTR: That is always the problem. People use different methods; you can ask wise people; you can write down all the positives and the negatives. But the future is not something you can see. So, therefore, you have to kind of take a risk. And you will never know if you really made the right choice or not, because you will never know what would have actually happened if you had chosen the other options. It may have looked as if what would have happened would not have been that good, but it is not necessarily the case that it *would* have happened like that. And it is not possible to ever find out, even afterwards.

Karma and creating a path

If we can do something with our life to help a lot of people, that would be wonderful, we can do that. That would also bring us a true kind of happiness, because when we see that we have done something that helped a lot of people, we would feel joy and happiness that we had done something useful, something beneficial.

But even if we couldn't do that much to transform the world, to transform people's lives and change them for the better, if we have a good heart and a positive attitude and not too much negativity, and remain like that, with a kind heart and not too much attachment and aversion, we would not have done anything bad. We would have remained contented and joyful and have no regrets, so that at the end of our life we could look back and say, "I didn't transform the world, I didn't do many great things, but at least I kept a good heart, a kind heart, and didn't do too many bad things. So, I can be content and go peacefully and happily."

We talk about karma in this context. The word karma means *the power of action*. It is very simple actually: How I am now is due to the karma of the past. If you want to know how you were in the past, you don't have to ask any special 'seers' or astrologers, or consult any kind of divination, you just have to look at yourself and see how you are. Because the way you are now is the result of all your past. It is also said that if you want to know how you will be in the future, again you don't have to ask anybody, not the seers or astrologers or consult any kind of divination. You just look at what you are doing, how you are reacting and behaving, how your mind is; if you see this, then you will know what your future will be. It is that simple; that is karma.

Sometimes people ask, "Is karma predestined or is there free will?" This is not the question. This is only asked by people who don't understand karma. There is nothing 'predestined' or 'not predestined,' everything is always changing. It's not like: 'This is my karma, signed, sealed, finished, done.' There is nothing like that. As you go, you change. Therefore, there is nothing called 'predestined.' But there is nothing called totally 'free will,' either. How you are is because of all the ways you have been. So, everything you do has an impact on what you are, and that is karma. It is the same with everything. The world is how it is now because of what we did in the past. So, if you want to make it better, you can make it better, but it is not going to happen overnight. We have to work step by step and solve each problem one by one.

So that is karma. It is nothing mysterious. It is just simple cause and effect. If we have some understanding of this then how to work with it becomes clear. You know what you have to do. You have to work on yourself, or train yourself: your mind, your emotions, and your reactions.

The Buddhist view talks about Two Truths, which are the Relative Truth and the Ultimate Truth. [The understanding of these are what were referred to earlier as 'worldly wisdom' and 'transcendental wisdom,' respectively.] Relative Truth is what each of us experiences. Ultimate Truth is how things really are. So, therefore, the Ultimate Truth is very important. Mahamudra is about that, for example, to experience the Ultimate Truth, which will really free us. But we also have to take care of the Relative Truth, which is where we are now, how we act and react. These two things need to go together.

We need to notice and see how our mind is; how we are feeling, what emotions are going on, and what we are doing with our body, speech and mind. If we find we are doing something positive, we should congratulate ourselves. You have to appreciate yourself because nobody else is going to! If you want others to appreciate you, then you are in trouble, because they probably will not. So, it is important to appreciate it yourself, if you are doing something positive. But if you find you are doing something not-so-positive, then you can let it go; there is no need to do it. Because you are your own master, there is nobody who can force you to do something you do not choose to do.

In this way, you are practising dharma, you are transforming yourself. But then, in addition to this approach, in order to understand your true nature, you have to go a little bit deeper, which comes through meditation. This needs to be practised over time. Using both these approaches together creates a path. Slowly, slowly, not expecting too much, that is the way.

Through Mahamudra and meditation it is possible to find this way of being that we could call 'non-dualistic.' It is possible to come to experience how everything you experience is a manifestation, or a radiance, of your own mind. At that point, you find that you don't need to react with aversion and attachment. When you can truly experience that, then you no longer need to be afraid in any way. You don't have to feel bad or upset or angry or jealous or attached, or anything like that, because you understand how your experience is your own manifestation. And thereby, you can actually be totally free.

It takes time to truly experience this, but even to have a little bit of understanding, or sometimes they say just to have heard this, can be very helpful. For example, as you die, whatever experiences you have at that time, you can know that it is all your own experience because nothing real is happening 'out there.' If you can understand this, then you can be free of fear and anger and attachment and jealousy and all these things. And if you are free of these, then you can be totally liberated.

If we can face things without too much worry and too much anxiety, life goes easier. If we have too much worry and stress, it makes our life go more heavily and with more difficulty. If we can go a little bit deeper, and deeper still, then eventually we can go beyond fear and hope; and that is what we call being enlightened. But in the first instance, just being a little bit lighter and freer in our lives is a good thing. That is why the journey of dharma is about being a little bit relaxed, and gradually working on our emotions and reactions and habitual tendencies. That is the practice; that is the path.

Foundational understanding

If we only go into deep, profound and complicated kinds of teachings and we never go into the simple and foundational type of teachings, it can sometimes lead to the misunderstanding that Buddhist practice is something that you have to do in a monastery or in retreat, in a place which is totally outside the scope of usual worldly life. It might give the impression it is not something we can practise in our daily life as an ordinary person doing all sorts of usual work, having a family, living in society and doing what is necessary for these. But it is not like this at all.

Buddhism should be possible to be practised anywhere; in daily life, as a householder, as a professional; as a person in whatever culture or society we are in, whether it is 'Eastern' or 'Western.' Mostly, it can be practised simply by being a good human being. This is what the Buddha taught, for the main part, and it describes a way of life that is quite simple and doesn't necessarily require lots of prayers or rituals or even too much special time put aside for a lot of meditation.

Wherever I go and whatever I teach, I always try and emphasize this. Any kind of practices, or whatever texts we learn from, they need to be integrated into our life. They have to be something that we can use in our daily life. This is the case with the Eightfold Path. This path comes from the Four Noble Truths, which is the basic teaching of the Buddha and actually includes all the teachings of the Buddha. The Buddha never taught anything else except the Four Noble Truths. Everything else the Buddha taught is an expansion, an elaboration, of the Four Noble Truths.

I have been travelling in the West trying to talk about Buddhism since Christmastime, 1989. Over this time, I have travelled for months and months every year and taught all sorts of things. My archive-keeper told me recently, she has thousands of hours of recordings of me talking! And what I feel is that most of the time, I have been trying to clear up misunderstandings. There are so many instances of half-information or where information is not completely clear in people's minds, about many things.

I think this happens when the foundation of understanding is not so clear, not so strong. So, there is nothing wrong with repeating things. It is all about repetition in dharma - the practice is and the teaching is also, because it can take time for things to be understood fully.

When the foundation is clear, then everything becomes clear. When the foundation is not clear, then nothing is clear, everything gets a little bit complicated. Many questions arise, which are often best answered by clarifying the basics.

Three sacred principles

We talk about Three Sacred Principles in Buddhism, as a kind of daily practice. The first principle is to watch our motivation. When you get up, or at any time, whatever you are doing, you consider why you are doing it; with what intention you are doing it. If I am doing something to deliberately do something wrong or harmful, or with too much selfish motivation, I notice that and notice it is not that great. If I can do something with a compassionate and wise motivation, then it is very good. This is the attitude of a Bodhisattva, a very positive, very powerful, and very compassionate attitude. We can always change our motivation. So, this is the first principle; to see our motivation and make it correct, positive.

Then, secondly, whatever actions we do, we see that we are not too aggressive or too attached, not too intense about things. Everything is impermanent, everything is changing. Nothing lasts, not even me. So, I don't have to be so upset or so attached to anything. I don't have to be so angry. Too much aversion or too much attachment creates negative things towards yourself and towards others. So, we try to lessen that.

Lastly, at the end of the day for instance, or if you are doing any kind of meditation practice, at the end of that, you dedicate it. This means that whatever result or positive karma comes out of that day or that practice or whatever, you give it for whatever purpose is your long-term goal. For example, you could wish that, "Whatever positive karma or positive results happen because of my actions today, may it go to help all sentient beings to be free from their suffering, so that they have lasting peace and happiness; I give it for that." This is like depositing any good results in another account, so it can't be lost. It is as if that account is very secure, it multiplies all the time, so the good results cannot be lost once you have done that. It is very positive.

Walking a Noble Path

Four Noble Truths

The Buddha taught Four Noble Truths:

There is suffering.
There is the cause of suffering.
There is the cessation of suffering
And there is the path to the cessation of suffering.

Then he said:
There is suffering; it has to be understood.
There is the cause of suffering, which has to be eliminated.
There is the cessation of suffering, which must be achieved.
There is the path to the cessation of suffering, which must be practised.

And then he said, again:
There is suffering; it has to be understood, but there is nothing to understand.
There is the cause of suffering, which has to be eliminated, but there is nothing to eliminate.
There is the cessation of suffering, which must be attained, but

there is nothing to attain.
There is the path to the cessation; it must be practised, but there is nothing to practise.

Taken from 'The Lazy Lama looks at the Four Noble Truths' by Ringu Tulku

Causes of suffering

What are the causes that bring problems of dissatisfaction, pain and difficulties for us? This is the Second Noble Truth of the Buddha. What Buddha said was something unusual. He said that the real causes of suffering or unhappiness are klesha and karma. What is klesha? Klesha is the Sanskrit word for negative emotions. A negative emotion means an emotion that brings dissatisfaction and discomfort to yourself and others. Klesha includes not only emotions but also any state of mind that brings problems for ourselves and others. Ignorance is also regarded as a klesha. When we talk about ignorance we mean confusion, not knowing what is what; lack of clarity of the mind; wrong perception of how things are; and not knowing what it is that I am.

Klesha refers to our reactions - negative reactions like violent feelings, anger, hatred and wanting to harm people; greed and attachment, holding onto something too much, miserliness and never being satisfied; pride and arrogance; jealousy and envy; all these kinds of reactions which bring the opposite of peace. They bring suffering for yourself and then also impose problems on others.

Sometimes these days, in this age of consumerism, the idea seems to be that greed is good. Advertising suggests you should never be satisfied with anything; they want you to go on consuming more and more and more. The more you buy, the better you are, because you are helping the economy. The more you buy, the more you produce. The more you produce, the more you buy. The more you work hard to buy those things, the more you buy. Then you have no time to do anything else but buy and produce and work, and however much you buy, the idea is you should never be satisfied with it. The 'latest' thing is the 'best.' If you are satisfied with a watch that is 10 years old, that would be of no use.

In a way, there is nothing wrong with all this; but in another way, it makes you very busy and never satisfied. And that is the problem. We would need a whole other world to provide all the raw materials so that all the people can be provided with all the new things that everybody should have and that are changing all the time. This approach is what is difficult for the world, our 'container.' And when we are never satisfied with anything, is it really happiness? Happiness is satisfaction, being happy with what I have. It is contrary to greed.

So, klesha is regarded as one important element that brings suffering. Secondly there is karma, and it is very important to understand karma in the right way. Karma means 'action,' which is part of 'cause and effect.' Whatever type of causes and conditions happen or are made, that kind of reaction or result or situation is what will follow. Every situation that is happening now has its causes. Nothing happens without causes and conditions. It is not about everything being 'my fault' or that everything is a 'reward' or a 'punishment.' It is not like that.

Karma is about everything having its own causes and effects. It applies to me: my own actions have their reactions. Whatever I do and the way I live my life has consequences on my future days and my future life. What I do today, how I think today, how I live today, affects what I will experience tomorrow; sometimes in a big way, sometimes in a more individual way. What I do, not only with my body but also with my emotions and thoughts and mind, has an impact on how things will be.

This applies to a society or a family or a country. How a society will become depends on how people are and what we do. Karma does not mean something like: "I did something wrong in my last life and now I have the consequences, and there is nothing I can do." The word karma means the power of action. It actually means what I do matters. This responsibility is very important. How I act makes a big difference, if not to others at least very much to myself.

My future is made now. My future is not made in the past. My future is made now. My present was made in the past. If I just allow my present to take its own course, without trying to change it, then it will follow its course, and I allow the past to make my future as well. In this way, karma is very important. It can perpetuate suffering or it can be a force for change.

The Eightfold Path and Right View

The Buddha taught the Eightfold Path as a means of freeing ourselves from the causes of suffering, klesha and karma. The eight aspects of the path are:

- Right or 'Perfect' View
- Right Thought
- Right Speech
- Right Action
- Right Livelihood
- Right Effort
- Right Mindfulness
- Right Concentration

The path starts with 'Right View' and this covers everything from the very simplest right view to the most profound and deepest enlightened view. To have the complete understanding of the nature of reality and the nature of mind, and thereby to have complete realisation, this is Right View. Right View extends to this. But also, to have a very clear understanding that, whatever I do, I must do to others what I would like others to do to me; this is also Right View. I think Right View starts here. If I want people to be kind to me and compassionate to me and act respectfully towards me, then I should start to act like that myself, as well. If I have that understanding then I have a basic Right View.

What I want in life is what everybody wants. It is not good to do anything that would bring destructive and negative effects to others. Such acts would also bring negative effects to myself through karmic consequences. How I act and what I do affects others and also affects myself. This kind of understanding is sometimes called the 'Worldly' or 'Samsaric' Right View.

Worldly Right View is not necessarily understanding emptiness and all these sorts of things. Buddha did not talk about emptiness too much right from the beginning. He actually was quite reluctant to talk about emptiness. It is sometimes said that when he first talked about emptiness, many of his monks vomited blood! – because it was too hard to take. There is a story like that. That is why it is usually said that he only taught emptiness and all the Prajnaparamita sutras later on and only to a group of 'advanced' monks. This was at what we call Vulture's Peak Mountain.

Mostly, Buddha talked about kindness - loving-kindness and compassion - and not to be too self-centred. He talked about *ego* a lot. Sometimes it is translated as *ego* or sometimes as *ego-clinging*. He also talked about *egolessness* and *selflessness*. It is important to clarify some of this. When you talk about *Atma* and *Anatma* it is a different thing. What we are talking about here, basically, is not saying that there is nothing called 'me' or no experience of 'me' or 'I.' It is not talking about that. Instead, it is asking, "What is the *nature* of this thing that we call 'I,' as if it is something totally solid and enduring?"

We can also talk about the *selflessness of phenomena*. Here we can already see plainly that phenomena are not existing and thinking, "I am this or that phenomena." What we are referring to is that all these things that I see and experience as things existing on their own, are not existing in the way I commonly assume them to. What Buddha was saying is that if we look deeply at everything we see as existing on its own, as something existing very solidly and independently, we will find these things are not existing *independently* but rather *dependently*.

In the same way, the way I feel myself to be one thing that is solid and separate from everything else is actually not very solid at all. I am also a very transient and dependently arising 'thing'. I am not independent. I am dependent on everything else around me. I cannot say 'this is me' and the rest is nothing to do with me. This is very different from what we call 'ego' in psychology. I think generally when people talk about ego in the West they are just talking about 'I.' And actually, I see lots of people who have the problem of not having enough ego. It is true. Some people have the problem of having too much ego and some people have the problem of having too little ego. Too little ego means a person is so confused that they cannot feel any strong volition like, "Yes, I want to do this." "I want to get this done." "I want to be happy." Instead, the person is not 'together' – has no confidence, no willpower, no motivation, no integrity.

Sometimes people say you have to get angry and when you get angry it creates some volition or will-power to get something done. When you have absolutely no energy and are very down and lost, it may be okay to say this. This is one level. When we talk about trying to reduce ego, we are talking about people who already have too much ego, who are saying, "I want, I want this, I want that."

We can see psychology basically as a system to try to make us into healthy samsaric beings. In fact, if I am not a healthy samsaric being then it is not possible to practise Dharma and transcend samsara. So first we have to become a normal, healthy samsaric being. If we are not even that, then to talk about emptiness and egolessness makes things even worse. Such a person already has no energy and no direction so then if we talk about egolessness it makes them feel even more 'spacey.' You don't feel empty or spacey when you understand emptiness. You feel totally free and joyful.

This has to be very clearly understood: first we cultivate a healthy samsaric ego or mind, with all the usual things we want and don't want. This may include wanting to become enlightened and wanting to do something good. That is okay. That is what psychology tries to bring out. Once you have that, then Dharma comes in. So, Dharma practice does not bring you to the wrong kind of egolessness, but to the right kind of egolessness, one that brings lasting peace and happiness to yourself and others because you understand how best to work with circumstances. You find it is not helpful to always say 'I, I, I.' You can be more peaceful in any situation because you are not so concerned about yourself. There is less ego and you can be more happy. It is not that you don't know who you are, not this kind of egolessness, but that you are much wiser. You know you want happiness but you have a clearer and wiser understanding of how things work. This kind of egolessness is regarded as a very important thing to understand for our happiness.

Humility

When we talk about any of the practices of Buddhism, we are talking about something that you start to learn and then you keep on learning more and more. It is not: "Now I have the Right View, finished!" I try instead to understand more and more, deeper and deeper. The learning process is something that never finishes, from the Buddhist point of view, until you become enlightened. Therefore, humility is regarded as very important. It is part of Right View.

From the Buddhist point of view, humility is very important because, if you are too arrogant and proud it is said you can never learn. If you are too 'full' – 'too full with air' – you cannot learn. If I am too arrogant, then I cannot see the positive qualities of others. As long as I cannot see the positive qualities of others, I cannot learn. What could I learn if I can't see anything good in anybody? The more I look for the positive qualities of others, the more I can see the positive qualities of others and the more I can learn of them. Having this understanding and way of being, or possessing this quality of looking for the positive quality of others, is called humility. Humility is a way of being that allows us to start to look for the positive qualities of others.

Usually, we look for the negative qualities of others: "Oh, he is a bit like that…, she is a bit like that…" It is very easy to pick up the faults of others. The good qualities that others have is often not the first thing that comes to mind. This is simply the habitual tendency we mostly have. And it is not a very good tendency because, if we are doing only that, then we are picking up bad qualities and we are not able to pick up any good qualities, because we don't see them. To have this understanding and attitude, to know arrogance and pride are a misguided way of acting, is the first and most important thing. We try firstly to see the positive qualities that are there. We don't have to pretend qualities are there that are not, but we look for positive qualities and when we see them, we notice them, we acknowledge them. The more we see positive qualities in others – because everybody has positive qualities – the more we can be aware of them and be respectful of that. It becomes the way in which we look at things.

A 'good' person and a 'bad' person comes down to this: a wise person sees good qualities and the good sides of everything. Seeing things this way, you can learn more. You receive more positive things. You become more positive. You are happier. You respect people much more, and other people appreciate you much more. Everything is better. If you are not so wise, then you notice only negative things, not the positive things. You are unhappy because you don't like people and people don't like you. You don't inherit any positive qualities from other people, only negative qualities, because you see only that. Then you say everybody is terrible, everything is bad. You think, "I am the only one who is good, but nobody sees it!" And then you are not happy.

Therefore, this kind of humility is a very important part of the right view. I am not talking here about all the different aspects of Right View but this is one aspect. The point is to develop these kinds of qualities, this way of seeing and understanding. We develop them in ourselves and work on this to start to develop Right View, which is then the strongest basis of all the other aspects of the Eightfold Path, like Right Action and so on.

Right Thought

Right Thought is the second aspect of the Eightfold Path. In Tibetan, the words which are translated as 'Thought' here include not only thoughts but also emotions. Any kind of thoughts, concepts, emotions and feelings, anything that arises in your mind, is included here. So, first we can look at unhelpful or negative emotions and then look at helpful or 'right' ones, and see how we can try to cultivate these.

We do not want suffering, unhappiness and problems. Therefore, anything that brings unhappiness and suffering or problems for ourselves or for others, by us or through us, we call 'negative' or 'unwholesome.' Anything that brings the opposite - happiness and satisfaction and the end of problems for ourselves and for others - is called 'right' or 'wholesome' or 'positive.' This is the general way of defining what is 'right,' or otherwise. From the Buddhist point of view, any kind of thoughts or emotions that disturb the mind are called negative: this includes anything that does not bring peace, tranquillity and joy but brings disturbance and thereby creates tension and dissatisfaction; anything that brings pain and hurt and unwholesome feeling and experience is considered negative. Those thoughts and emotions that cause us to act in a way that would be destructive, violent, or harmful to others, are called negative or unhelpful emotions.

Generally, from the Buddhist point of view, we talk about three mind poisons or sometimes five mind poisons. These are the main states of mind which are the basis of all the unwholesome arisings. It does not mean that these cover everything, but everything that arises and is unwholesome or negative is connected with these mind states, and falls into these groups. The three main, or root, mind poisons are: ignorance, aversion and attachment.

Ignorance is very broad. It includes many aspects: it is basically a confused state of mind. Your mind becomes unclear, kind of 'smoky;' not clear about what is going on. It has lots of doubts and does not know how things really are, which therefore creates a lot of fear. Because it is unclear, sometimes you have the wrong understanding, or misunderstandings or unclear understandings. You may hold on to things that are not even there. Ignorance has this aspect where you see something that is actually a shadow, for instance, but you think it is a demon and you hold on to that idea. Any thoughts or emotions or ways of seeing that are opposite or contrary or other than the way the situation actually is, is seen as ignorance. Ignorance is regarded as the basis of all wrong thoughts.

Fundamentally, ignorance is holding on to a view of things, including 'myself,' as totally separate and totally solid and independent from everything else. The dualistic view comes from experiencing myself in this way. Once I see myself as "This is me," that I am solid and separate from everything around me, I am also assuming that "This is me here and everything else is out there." If one has this way of looking, then all other problems come, because I see myself as separate. So, it becomes that I am here and the rest of the world is there. With this way of seeing, I then must react to everything 'out there' as either something 'good for me' or 'not good for me.' If I see something as good for me, then I feel I must try to get it or hold on to it. If I see something as not good for me, then I feel I must try to get rid of it or run away from it. So, seeing things like this, I am naturally always reacting with attachment or aversion.

And yet, I cannot do as I am trying to do. I cannot actually get and hold onto everything that seems nice to me. Everything changes. So, there is nothing that you can really get and keep. When I say "I must get; I must have; I must hold on to..." etc., I cannot do so, because I am always changing; everything is always changing. Therefore, it is not possible to do that and I necessarily get into problems and unhappiness because I am trying to do something that is not possible for me to do.

It is the same way if I feel I have to get rid of something or run away from everything that I don't like or don't want. It is also not possible, because it is not under my control. Regardless of what I do, things come and things happen that I don't want. The more I don't want something, the more it appears to come, more strongly and closer by. The more I am like this, the more I don't want everything that is not nice and the more I want everything that is nice, the more the three mind poisons arise and the more problems I have. At the extreme I can even get into psychological illness.

In order to have even a healthy *samsaric* mind, you need to have some degree of balance – some degree of acceptance of having some things that are not nice and acceptance of not having some things you want. Otherwise, the situation becomes completely mad with too many problems and confusion. Some people can even get into a situation where they cannot leave their own room - everything has become fearful because it is not as they wish. There are different degrees of aversion and attachment. How much you are obsessed with this shows how stable your mind is and how happy you are. If you are really overly sensitive and cannot bear to have unpleasant things and must have only nice things, the more unhappy and unbalanced you will be. You have more problems and more negative emotions and suffer more strongly. Therefore ignorance, that kind of ignoring how things are, is what generates samsara.

From the Buddhist point of view, what transcends samsara is to understand very clearly that what I am, is not totally separate from everything else. What I am is not a totally independent thing, unrelated with everything. I am a relative thing, relative with everything around me - everything around me is also, in a way, part of me. I am a product of everything that goes around in the world. I am not one thing. I am changing. My body is not one thing. My body is a compounded thing. It changes, moment by moment. It is made of the environment I am in. It cannot be completely separated from the environment around me.

His Holiness Karmapa gave this example: He said that, if I were a totally independent thing, then I should be able to survive without breathing in and out. Because every time I breathe in, I breathe in the air that is around me. Then when I breathe out, I breathe out into the air around me. If I don't receive any air from outside for even a few minutes, then I am no longer there. So, how dependent am I on everything around me? I cannot survive, I no longer exist, if all the elements around me are not there. So, therefore, I am part of everything. I cannot survive otherwise. That is from a very gross way of looking. Not only the body, but everything I am, is a very interdependent thing. My body is not something totally separate or totally independent. But this is even more true for my mind. My mind changes all the time. One thought comes. It goes. One emotion comes; and goes. It is changing all the time. The one thing I think I am is not one thing; it is changing. This moment of 'me' – which is a very compounded thing – creates the next moment of 'me.' And that creates the next moment. Therefore, it is a continuum – it is not one thing; it is a continuum.

Change and continuity

From the Buddhist point of view, when we talk about life after life we do not mean it is something like a person changing clothes, moving from one life to the next. It is *not* as if in this life I have this body, these clothes, and then I take off these clothes and put on new clothes and that is my next life. Nor is it like a mala [a rosary of prayer beads], with many beads on one continuous string, like different lives, where 'I' go from this life to the next life, or from this moment to the next moment, or from yesterday to today, as the same thing, as one thing, a solid thing that is me, while my body is something else. The Hindu way of understanding life after life is more like that. But if you go deeply into Buddhist understanding, that is not what Buddhism says.

In Buddhist understanding, the connection between the body and mind is not just like between a person and their clothes. It is much stronger. Everything, the mind, the body and the whole system altogether is changing, with this moment creating the next moment, and so on. There is a continuum. There are five examples which are traditionally given to try to explain this:

- milk becoming yoghurt
- a face and its reflection
- the flame of one lamp to another
- a seal (or signet)
- a recitation, where I say something and you remember it, like a mantra

Therefore, it is not like there is one 'string' or one thing that is 'me' or 'my mind', and then every one of 'my' lives is like one bead on that string. It is not like that, because everything changes together. This is the way that milk becomes yoghurt – it is a continuum, with milk *itself* becoming yoghurt. The 'next life' of milk is yoghurt. But milk is milk and yoghurt is yoghurt. Milk is not yoghurt and yoghurt is not milk. When it is yoghurt, it is yoghurt and not milk. When it is milk, it is milk and not yoghurt. There is nothing like, "There is a thing called milk and now the thing that is milk has left and has entered into the yoghurt." It is nothing like that. It is not like something takes off the milk characteristics and enters into the yoghurt characteristics. It is not like that. It is just that, itself, it transforms.

In the same way, the change from one lifetime to another is not that there is one thing that goes into another. It *transforms*. In one way, what I am is not a solid form - it is emptiness, because there is nothing there that I can identify and hold on to and say, "This is me. This is the essence of me." There is nothing I can really pinpoint in this way. In a sense, the way I am is a very strange thing. There is an awareness but that awareness is not a thing; it's more like space. When there is space, you cannot do anything to it. You cannot erase the space. You cannot destroy the space. How could you destroy space when there is nothing there to destroy? Similarly, it is also impossible to completely diminish or destroy me, or my mind, because there is nothing there.

That is why sometimes people say it is all like an illusion. The world is like an illusion. I am like an illusion - *like* an illusion. What does this mean? An illusion is when it looks as if it is there but actually it is not there. It looks like you can see it but if you try to find the thing you see, you cannot find it. That is an illusion. 'I' am like an illusion means I am there but there is also nothing really there to find, because it is like space. And just as you cannot destroy an illusion, you cannot destroy mind. In that nothingness, in that emptiness, in that illusion, there is also an indestructibleness.

Therefore, we always talk in Buddhist terms about emptiness, interdependence, and relativeness, and about everything being like an illusion. That emptiness, the illusory nature of things, and impermanence, are all connected; they have to be understood as one thing. But at the same time, we also talk about *vajra* nature, or our Buddhanature, as being vajra-like, which means indestructible. It is indestructible because there is nothing to destroy.

Vajra nature is not indestructible because there is *something there* which cannot be destroyed. There are lots of debates about this. For example, is there nothing there or is there something like a clear light, or awareness, which cannot be destroyed? But these two ways of asking the question are not actually two different things. If you really understand it, they come to the same thing; there is no difference because of the way things exist. Because it is emptiness, there is nothing there, no form, nothing you can hold on to in any way. Therefore, it is indestructible. So, the clear light, our awareness, is something very strange. It is illusion-like. It is not 'there' but because it is illusion-like, it cannot be 'disappeared.' Awareness is like that. You cannot say it is separate from everything else because it is not a thing. It is also not something that is together with everything else, because there is no thing. It is all illusion-like. If we see this we can relax more.

If we really know how to let be, it is not necessary to have all our fear and aversion and attachment that we live with, because nothing matters so much: whether you have everything that you want, or you have everything that you don't want, it doesn't matter, because there is nothing concretely there that is always beneficial or not. You cannot get rid of anything because there is no thing there. It is an illusion. It is a misunderstanding. It is a wrong view. I think, 'I need this' or 'I don't need this.' But all this attachment and fear is based on a deep misconception. And that is the difference between samsara and enlightenment; it is based on how you see yourself.

Love and attachment

Love and attachment are very different things. Greed, craving and attachment are about feeling "I want this; I have to have this." We are talking about any state which brings a strong sense of "If I don't have this, then I cannot be happy." There are many different degrees of this, of course, but when I talk about attachment, I am talking about feeling "I like this; I want this; I need this." 'I' is the primary thing. This is how we see it from the Buddhist point of view, at least, and that this becomes a source of problems. 'I' get attached. I crave for it, whatever it is. If it is there, I feel a little bit good but it also brings all sorts of problems because if it is not there, I feel I must get it. I feel I have a lack of it. Even when it is there, I have fear of losing it. If I lose it, I feel very bad because I have lost something I want. So, with attachment the mind becomes disturbed by lots of worries and tension.

Love, strictly speaking, from the Buddhist point of view, is about others. It is about the welfare of others. I wish this person, or those people, well. The welfare and benefit of those people is utmost in my mind. That is love. That is compassion. The more I feel like that, the less I am bothered about whether I have something in particular or not. My motivation is more about others. When that kind of loving-kindness is there, it does not have to manifest with attachment or aversion. Rather, there can be a very pure love, which brings open-minded and beneficial ways of thinking. And this kind of love brings peace to my mind, satisfaction to my mind, and joy to my mind.

This kind of love may also manifest within a samsaric state of mind, in which case it comes together with aversion and attachment. Then it may bring pain as well. How painful love is depends on how great the 'samsaric portion' is within it. Love can be painless and joyful, clear and open. Love can also be a little bit painful and tense. And this depends on which portion is greater: the purity of the love or the samsaric attachment and aversion.

Compassion becomes very important when working with attachment because compassion is the opposite of all the negative ways of feeling. Instead of feeling greed, always 'I want, I want…,' with compassion it is possible to feel more generosity, contentment and satisfaction. For example, I see a flower and it is very nice. Maybe it belongs to someone else, but I do not need to feel jealous, I don't have to own it. I can simply enjoy it, as it is. I can appreciate it. It is a wonderful flower, nicely arranged, belonging to that person – very nice. When I can feel like that, I am being healthy and I feel content. Contentment is appreciating something. I can be happy that somebody has that nice flower, I can wish that for everybody. If I have one, that is very good. But if I don't have one, at least I can still look at one. I can still rejoice in it and that is the same as having one. We don't always have to be jealous and greedy.

Greed is a never-fulfilling pit of fire. Fire is something that, whatever you put in, it gets burned up. The more you put in, the more the fire burns. You can never get rid of the fire by putting lots of things in it. The only way you can get rid of the burning sensation of the fire is not to put any more wood in it or anything to burn in it. Desire and greed are like that. You can never fulfil them by feeding them more things. The only way to end the cycle is to change your way of looking, and to stop feeding the greed. Mahatma Gandhi said many times, "In this world we have enough resources to fulfil the needs of every person. But we will never have enough resources to satisfy the greed of anybody, not even one person." Because greed is like that, it is always wanting more.

People often don't understand that greed is a painful thing. They think of it as an interesting thing, or an exciting thing. But if you look deeply you see it is a painful thing. Because unfulfilled desire is painful. And the more greed you have, the more unfulfilled you are. It is never enough. You have a poverty state of mind. The main understanding from the Buddhist point of view is that contentment is the essence of richness.

Right Speech

All sentient beings are similar in wanting to be happy and in trying to get happiness. What basically differentiates a human being from other beings, is speech, mainly. In the Tibetan way of thinking, the characteristic of a human being is 'someone who can talk and who understands when other people are talking;' and that is a 'human being' among the beings. So, therefore, speech is a very important aspect of our special qualities or special way of being among the sentient beings.

Speech can also be very negative and bring problems and harm to others and to ourselves. We therefore have to understand what 'wrong' speech is and what 'right' speech is, and try to work on that. Wrong speech, as we generally understand it, is false speech – telling lies. There are usually four aspects of negative speech described:

- Telling lies
- Speech that brings discord and disharmony among people
- Harsh words or speech that brings pain and hurt to people
- Gossiping

I am not sure if 'gossiping' is the right word to use. The fourth aspect of negative speech is speech that generates discomfort and negative emotions in people. The word translates to mean speech that generates negative thoughts and emotions in people's minds. It also kills people's useful time. But, overall, these are the four aspects of negative speech.

Telling lies means you know what is true but you want to give the wrong information in order to deceive people. Lies mean deceiving: you want to give the wrong information and not help people have the right understanding of things. When you tell a lie, immediately you feel a little bit uncomfortable because you know you are doing something wrong. It is easy to tell that somebody is telling a lie, because you know the way he is saying something is a little bit uncomfortable. Deceiving people is basically trying to harm people. It is trying to get some advantage for yourself. It does not bring good to yourself or to others.

One big problem with lies is that most of the time if you tell a lie, it will be found out, sooner or later. And when people find out the lie, the person who is telling the lie will never be trusted. So maybe you try to do something to deceive people so as to get some benefit or advantage for the time being, but in the long term you are creating a situation where nobody can trust you. When nobody can trust you, you have no worth. When people know you are not telling the truth and you are telling lies, whatever you later say, they are doubtful and don't know whether you are telling the truth or telling lies. Therefore, people don't trust you. Which means your worth as a human being is not very much - because a human being's basic characteristic is that he / she can express things. But you have expressed things in a wrong way. So, therefore, telling lies is a very negative thing, not only for others but also for yourself.

Good communication

Question: You have been giving teachings about aversion and attachment, but isn't indifference worse than attachment and aversion? Isn't it worse to be indifferent to somebody than to have attachment or aversion to them? Because even when you have aversion to somebody, at least there is some kind of communication or dialogue, whereas with indifference there is no communication at all.

RTR: Indifference is a kind of ignorance. It is ignoring. In the samsaric state of mind it is said that we react in one of these three ways: attachment, aversion or indifference. With something that we feel is nice or good for us, we become attached. If we feel it is not good for us, then we react with aversion. Or, if it is neither of these, we ignore it. This is not necessarily only talking about how we react to people. It applies to everything that we see and experience.

When I react to people with aversion, there is a kind of fear or dislike, 'wanting to get out.' This is not communication. Aversion and attachment are not communication. They are my reaction. This is talking about my reaction, from my side only. Communication is another thing. We can communicate with people without aversion and also without attachment and without indifference. Communication is having an exchange of information and ideas; any exchange is communication. Of course, communication can be with a lot of aversion and attachment also, but it is not necessary that it has to be.

Indifference is when we don't react. When we don't react to something, at least it doesn't bring too many problems. We are not reacting with fear or hatred. In a way, it is neutral. So, it doesn't bring anything good, but it also doesn't bring anything negative. If we react with aversion and attachment, then it could bring something negative. If, on the other hand, we react with kindness, with compassion, with positive feeling, then this brings more positive things. So, therefore, the way we react can be positive, negative or no reaction.

Question: When you have to fight for a cause, sometimes you have to say unpleasant things to people. What should we do then?

RTR: Can you give an example?

Question: There was a public talk and someone was saying everyone had to pay but this was not possible for the poor people. I was there and I made the point that it was difficult to pay when you don't have much money in your pocket. But afterwards I was not feeling so good, from saying something so 'hard'. But sometimes it is necessary to say strong words.

RTR: I think you did very well. Why would you feel bad about it? Sometimes, you may want to make a point and say that people who have lots of money have no problem paying but those who don't may have. But I myself don't see any harsh words here. Or any lies or any creating of discordance. I don't see any negative thing in what you said. It is possible that you were kind of 'attacking' a little bit, so the people didn't feel that good afterwards. But I don't think you said anything too bad there.

Of course we have to say things. We have to speak. It is very important to mention though, that when we speak we need to try and speak the truth and avoid harsh words and things like that. To say something in an angry way usually doesn't work anyhow. Most of the time, in any kind of negotiation or any kind of debate, if you become emotional, angry and abusive, it doesn't create the right kind of impact. It creates the opposite. The more you are angry and emotional and kind of 'attacking' the other person, the more angry and defensive they become.

You cannot convince somebody through debating, by saying they are wrong. This is something I learnt from experience, a long time ago - although I still do it! If you really want to convince somebody, you have to make them say, 'Yes', 'Yes', 'Yes'. And then you can convince somebody of something. If you say, "No, it is not like that!" then the other person will say, "No, it is not like that!" Even if they really agree, they won't want to agree with you then. Even if you have all the right logic, the other person won't want to accept your point of view. Therefore, if you really want to convince somebody, you need to make them say, 'Yes,' rather than, 'No.' One 'yes' to another 'yes' to another 'yes' – then you can come to the same conclusion. That is said to be the best way. And it is actually so.

By arguing you cannot convince anybody. We have so much pride that if somebody is trying to show us the opposite view, we will always want to defend our own view. And we will want to defend it to the last. Whatever may be said, I won't want to listen or give in. This is something we can see about human nature generally. We need to keep it in mind when we speak about things. But I think it is very important to speak up against injustice, against atrocities, against untruth. Otherwise, it is not much use that we can speak. We might as well be the same as cows or other animals who cannot speak then.

TIME AND SPACE

Question: Can you explain something about time and space, how they exist? I read something saying that time and space don't really exist. But I don't understand; if time and space do not exist, then how can people go to the past or go to the future?

RTR: What it is saying, is this: Time is a relative thing. And space is a relative thing. Everything is a relative thing. When you say past, what is this 'past'?

Questioner: What has gone before.

RTR: But past is relating to the present. Past is past, only in relation to the present. We say this is the present ... and now ... it is past. We call it the past because it is relating to the present. If we don't have a present, we cannot call anything past. Past and future are both relating to a present. This present is 'our present,' my experience, this is present. Therefore, there was past and there will be future.

In time itself, what is past and what is future? There is no past or future, because past and future are only in relation to the present. This is in the same way as how everything is relative. What is big and what is small, for example? How big is 'big'? If you say, "This is small and this is big," the two things depend on each other as to which is the big one and which is the small one. If you change one thing, maybe the first thing is now big in relation to that, whereas it was small in relation to the other thing. What is fast and what is slow? What is good and what is not good? Everything is relative.

Therefore, it is not saying that time and space do not exist, but that it is all relative. Nothing is existing as something on its own. There is nothing we can point to and say, always, 'this is the past.' Relating to this, this is past; relating to something else, this is present; relating to something else, this is future. Therefore, the past becomes the future and the future can become 'past' in relation to something else. There is nothing called the past on its own. The past is the past because of its relationship to the present moment.

Therefore, if I think about something, like when I was a little child, then that was the past. It is not actually 'past' necessarily, it is just being a little child. If I think about something where I am even older than I am now, with no teeth left or anything, that time is then my future.

Space is the same. What is 'space'? There is no thing called 'space.' This here is space. But what is it? There is nothing here. Space is a name for nothing. Now, if we put walls we can call this space inside the walls, a room. But space is not here because of 'space' but because of the walls. Space is the space between the four walls. But actually, there is no thing there. Is 'space' there? What is there? What is space? Space is only when there is nothing there, that is the space. There is only this wall here and that wall there and, therefore, this is a room. The space is here because of that – "I have lots of space here" – but actually I don't have anything here. So, space does not exist, on its own.

Questioner: What is it that exists, then, between the stars and the planets?

RTR: Nothing.

Questioner: Why is it coloured then?

RTR: Because of eyes. Because we have eyes and because of the way our eyes see. The colour is not there on the thing. Colour exists in the way light radiates and because of the way our eyes are. We see colour because of how our eyes are. It is not there, in itself. If you want to understand this, you just have to study a little physics to know very clearly about these things.

Questioner: They say they don't know what is between the stars and the planets.

RTR: Because there is nothing! Well, there could be something, I don't know. But space is space. By the definition of space, it is nothing. Where there is the possibility of having anything – precisely because there is nothing - there is the space. In Tibetan we say, in translation something like:

> "The characteristic of space is like a vacuum,
> where anything can happen"

When we talk about things not existing on their own, in the way they truly exist, it does not mean there is nothing happening, that nothing is experienced. In order to understand this element of Buddhist philosophy, it is very important that the understanding of the interdependence of things, and of emptiness, come together. It is the understanding of these two, together, that allows you to understand how time and space exist.

From the Buddhist point of view, we see that the nature of everything is emptiness; and because of that way of existing, everything is interdependent. Because everything is interdependent, or dependently-arising, therefore there is emptiness. And therefore, everything is possible. Any kind of manifestations are possible. Manifestations are always possible. It is not possible to have no manifestations, there is no stop to them, because of emptiness. If something was existing totally on its own, independently, then it would not be possible to change it because of how it was existing on its own. Its conditions cannot change if it exists on its own. But because nothing exists on its own, everything can be affected by everything. And everything can, therefore, change.

Also, everything can affect other things. This gives rise to all the chemistries and reactions, the creation of all the cosmos and the changing of all the cosmos; from the biggest level of the cosmos down to the atomic and subatomic level – all these possibilities of creating lots of things, and the dissolving of them, is all due to this way of how things exist.

The way I am is also part of this whole, creating situation. The way you and I see everything is like, 'This is a room. This is a picture on the wall. This is the world and it is truly here.' But is it? This picture, is it exactly like I see it, or not? I see the picture. You see the picture. But how would it be if somebody came along who had slightly different eyes to the kind of eyes that we have, for example? To use a very simple example, as if they had x-ray eyes? If someone had eyes like an x-ray, would they see this picture? They would not see this picture. I don't know exactly what they would see, but they would not see the picture I do now. That does not mean they would be seeing it wrongly. We are seeing the picture the way it is from our perspective. It is one way of seeing and it is right. But another way of seeing is not wrong. It is just another way of seeing.

So, therefore, it is possible that the same thing, when we look at it, can be seen as many different things by different people. The way I see the picture - and the way I see the world around me - is interdependently-arising. It is partly because of the way I am. If I didn't have this kind of brain, this kind of neurological system, this kind of eye, I would not see it this way. Therefore, this world would be totally different for somebody who was totally different to me. So then, which of these two different worlds is the real one? There is nothing called 'the real one,' in that way we commonly assume things are.

Now, going to the past and going to the future is another thing. Whether I can really go into the past or into the future is another story. Past has already happened. It is not there. Can I go back to yesterday? Yesterday is not there anymore. Can I go into tomorrow? Tomorrow is not there. But it may be possible that I have some kind of *experience* of yesterday, or of tomorrow. Or maybe of the next century. I could maybe experience something like that. But it is not that 'I am going there.' It is just one of my experiences.

Questioner: Can your mind go there?

RTR: I could call it my mind going into the future. But actually, the future is not there. It is just that I am having an experience that is yet to come. You cannot really go *into* the future, because the future is not there, so where would you go? That is how the world is relative. It is not solid. It is not existing in only one way. Time is also not existing in one way or solid, because past is gone. It is not there, nowhere to go. Future is not there, nothing to come, nowhere to go. Even present has nowhere to go. Because what is present? It is something that is constantly changing. Where is the present? Now, this is the present but if you try to catch the present, it is difficult. Is it now?…now?…now? You cannot catch the present.

A professor of mathematics from Oxford University once explained to me that he can mathematically prove emptiness. You cannot find the present, because you cannot find a minimum time interval, in the same way as you cannot find a minimum measurement of space. For example, this is one metre. One metre can be divided into many centimetres. Each centimetre can be divided into millimetres and each millimetre can be divided many times. However small the measurement, there is nothing you cannot divide further. There is no limit at which you can mathematically find the smallest division; whether it is time you are considering, whether it is space, or whether it is anything. There is no smallest thing that you can say, 'this is the minimum unit that exists.'

Therefore, when exactly is the existing present moment? Or when is the smallest moment? There is no one precise moment we can point to. There is no present moment. When there is no present moment, there cannot be any past or future, as something separately existing. So, therefore, it is all interdependent. Relatively, time is there. But ultimately, there is no time there. In the same way: relatively, everything is there; but ultimately, nothing is there. It is all dependently and interdependently existing: emptiness *and* appearance. This is how it is for everything.

Questioner: When we talk about individual streams of consciousness, when do they touch and how are they separate from one another? If an individual stream of consciousness is like a river, does that have borders or shores? Does it sometimes touch another river, another stream of consciousness, or does it always remain separate?

RTR: It is just defined as my experience. As long as I have this strong feeling that 'I am,' then I have this sense of continuous experience: yesterday was me, today is me, tomorrow will be me. There is a continuum. This is my experience. It is not necessarily there if I look from an outside point of view, but experientially it is there.

It is not like, "Yesterday I was Ringu Tulku but today I feel like Gaby." There is a kind of a continuum. But this is not saying that exactly the same thing is existing, day to day, moment to moment.

There is not one thing existing. In a way, it doesn't exist on its own because yesterday's 'me' is not today's 'me.' Yesterday's 'me' is different from today's 'me' because every moment things change. My body changes; my thoughts change; my emotions change. Everything changes but there is this kind of a continuum. This is how it feels, so there is a continuum - of experience - for an individual.

As for this 'me,' where is the boundary? Is there a distinct boundary? Maybe that kind of boundary becomes something different when you become enlightened, because they say you can become countless beings when you become enlightened, if you want to. I am not saying anything from my own experience, I am just quoting from the teachings. The more realised you become, the more beings you can emanate. So, when you are a Buddha, the number is countless. Therefore, there is no longer only one being. That sense of "I am only one," slowly dissolves. You know that there is nothing that you need to hold onto that is 'me.' Though from the experiential point of view, there is a feeling and experience of a continuum.

Questioner: Even between lives?

RTR: Yes, because otherwise there is no continuum. Like yesterday and today. Yesterday and today are different but there is a continuum. The causes and conditions that created today come from yesterday and from the day before. In the same way, the causes and conditions of the way I am, have come from my past life, and will lead to my future life. Each life, and each moment, are not exactly the same, but there is a continuum.

Dedication

All my babbling,
In the name of Dharma,
Has been set down faithfully
By my dear students of pure vision.

I pray that at least a fraction of the wisdom
Of those enlightened teachers
Who tirelessly trained me
Shines through this mass of incoherence.

May the sincere efforts of all those
Who have worked tirelessly
Result in spreading the true meaning of Dharma
To all who are inspired to know.

May this help dispel the darkness of ignorance
In the minds of all living beings
And lead them to complete realisation
Free from all fear.

                                                  Ringu Tulku

Glossary

Attachment refers to grasping, holding on too strongly to something, clinging to it; you get too close to something you perceive as 'nice' until your relating with it takes on a 'sticky' kind of feeling.

Aversion refers to a mind quality of rejecting or pushing something away; wishing it were not there; trying to eliminate it or get away from it.

Bodhicharyavatara (Sanskrit) also known as *The Bodhisattvacharyavatara* is an 8th century Mahayana text, outlining the path of the Bodhisattva. It was composed by Shantideva, a great scholar, at the famous Nalanda Monastery in Northern India. It found wide acclaim almost immediately in India and rapidly spread. It was translated into Tibetan during the 9th century. It is the key text for anyone following the Bodhisattvayana (Mahayana) path. There are many translations into English from several languages. One is *The Bodhisattva's Way of Life* translated by the Padmakara Translation Group from Tibetan, revised edition: Shambhala 2006.

Bodhicitta (*Bodhichitta* Sanskrit; *chang chub kyi sem* Tibetan) is the heart essence of the Buddha, of enlightenment. The root of the word, Bodh, means 'to know, to have the full understanding' and *citta* refers to the heart-mind or 'heart feeling.' In a practical sense, Bodhicitta is compassion: compassion imbued with wisdom.

Bodhisattva (Sanskrit; *changchub sempa* Tibetan) comes from the root *bodh* which means to know, to have the full understanding. The term describes a being who has made a commitment to work for the benefit of others to bring them to a state of lasting peace and happiness and freedom from all suffering. A Bodhisattva does not have to be a Buddhist but can come from any spiritual tradition or none. The key thing is that they have this compassionate wish to free all beings from suffering, informed by the wisdom of knowing this freedom is possible.

Buddhanature / Buddha nature (*Sugatagarba* Sanskrit; *desheg nyingpo* Tibetan) refers to the fundamental, true nature of all beings, free from all obscurations and distortions. Ultimately, our true nature and the true nature of all beings is inseparable from the nature of Buddha. It is the 'primordial goodness' of sentient beings, an innate purity and clarity of mind and heart.

Dharma (Sanskrit; *chö* Tibetan) The word dharma has many uses. In its widest sense, it means all that can be known, or the way things are. The other main meaning is the teachings of the Buddha; also called the *Buddhadharma*. The *Buddhadharma* refers to the entire body of oral and written Buddhist teachings, and includes the literal teachings and that which is learnt through practising them.

Eightfold Path or **Noble Eightfold Path** describes 'the path of noble beings' to freedom from suffering. It is the fourth of The Four Noble Truths initially taught by the Buddha. The path of practice he laid out is the cultivation and perfection of the eight related aspects: Right or 'perfect' View, Thought, Speech, Action, Livelihood, Effort, Mindfulness and Concentration.

Emptiness (*shunyata* Sanskrit; *tong pa nyi* Tibetan) The Buddha taught in the second turning of the wheel of Dharma, that all phenomena have no real, independent existence of their own. They only appear to exist as separate, nameable entities because of the way we commonly, conceptually, see things. But in themselves, all things are 'empty' of inherent existence. This includes our 'self,' which we habitually, unconsciously, mistake to be an independently-existing, separate phenomenon. Instead, everything exists in an interdependent way and this is what the term emptiness refers to. As Ringu Tulku says in *Like Dreams and Clouds* Bodhicharya Publications: 2011: "Emptiness does not mean there is nothing; emptiness means the way everything is, the way everything magically manifests."

Freda Bedi (1911 – 1977) was a British woman from Derby. She went to St Hugh's College, Oxford University, and married an Indian scholar who she met while studying at Oxford. She lived in India from her mid-20's, working tirelessly in a number of activist, humanitarian and socio-political roles. She had four children, was an active force in the struggle for Indian Independence led by Mahatma Gandhi, and later became the first Western woman to become a fully ordained Tibetan Buddhist nun, under His Holiness the 16th Karmapa. To read more about her life see, for example: '*The Revolutionary Life of Freda Bedi: British feminist, Indian nationalist, Buddhist nun*' by Vicki Mackenzie.

Kagyu (Tibetan) *Ka* means 'oral' and *gyu* means 'lineage:' the lineage of oral transmission, also known as the 'Lineage of Meaning and Blessing' or the 'Practice Lineage'. It traces its origins to the primordial Buddha, Dorje Chang (Vajradhara) and the great Indian master and yogi, Tilopa. It is one of the four major schools of Tibetan Buddhism, and is headed by His Holiness the Karmapa, currently H.H. XVII Karmapa Ogyen Trinley Dorje. The other three main schools are the Gelug, Nyingma, and Sakya.

Karma (Sanskrit; *lay* Tibetan) literally means 'action.' It refers to the cycle of cause and effect that is set up through our actions. Actions coloured or motivated by *klesha* (see below), for example, anger or desire, will tend to create results in keeping with that action and also increase our tendency to do similar actions. These tendencies become ingrained in us and become our habitual way of being, which is our karma. With awareness, we can change our karma through consciously refining our actions.

Karmapa (Tibetan), *see Kagyu.*

Kleshas (Sanskrit; *nyön mong* Tibetan) are translated as mental defilements, mind poisons or negative emotions. They include any emotion or mind state that disturbs or distorts consciousness. They bring forth our experience of suffering and prevent our experience of love, joy and happiness. The three main kleshas are desire, anger and ignorance. Combinations of these give rise to the five kleshas, which are these three plus pride and envy / jealousy.

Lama (Tibetan; *guru* Sanskrit) means teacher or master. *La* refers to there being nobody higher in terms of spiritual accomplishment, and *ma* refers to being like a mother, having compassion like a mother. Thus, both wisdom and compassion are brought to fruition together in the lama. The word has the connotation of 'heavy' or 'weighty,' indicating the guru or lama is heavy with positive attributes and kindness.

Mahamudra (Sanskrit; *cha ja chen po* or *chak chen* Tibetan) literally means 'Great Seal' or 'Great Symbol', referring to the way in which all phenomena are 'sealed' by their primordially perfect, true nature. The term can denote the teaching, meditation practice or accomplishment of Mahamudra. The meditation consists in perceiving the mind directly rather than through rational analysis or conceptualisation, and relies on a direct introduction to the nature of the essence of the mind. This form of meditation is traced back to Saraha (10th century), and was passed down in the Kagyu school through Marpa. The accomplishment lies in experiencing the non-duality of the phenomenal world and emptiness: perceiving how the two are not separate. This experience can also be called the union of emptiness and luminosity.

Prajnaparamita Sutra (Sanskrit) is the sutra given by the Buddha on the sixth Paramita or 'perfection' of wisdom (*prajna* Sanskrit). *Jna* refers to 'knowledge' or 'understanding' and *pra* is an intensifier which denotes 'higher' or 'greater' or 'unsurpassed' knowing. It describes the wisdom of directly realising emptiness, the non-conceptual simplicity of all phenomena. There are many versions of these teachings, of varying lengths, and many translations into English from several languages.

Rinpoche (Tibetan) is an honorific term in the Tibetan Buddhist tradition, reserved for great masters. It refers to how precious it is that such teachers are among us; literally translating as 'precious one'.

Samsara / samsaric (Sanskrit; *khor wa* Tibetan) is the state of suffering of 'cyclical existence'. It describes a state of mind that experiences gross and / or subtle pain and dissatisfaction. It arises because the mind is deluded, confused and unclear and thus perpetually conditioned by habits of attachment, aversion and ignorance.

Tulku (Tibetan) is the title given to someone who has been recognized as the re-incarnation of a previous realised master or Lama.

Vajra (Sanskrit; *dorje* Tibetan) is sometimes translated as 'diamond-like.' It symbolises that which is indestructible, that which can cut through anything else but cannot, itself, be destroyed. The symbol is a ritual object like a kind of sceptre, made of metal. What it symbolises is the vajra state, attained through understanding the essence of mind as pure emptiness. Once this understanding is attained, we see that there is nothing that can be destroyed because everything exists in emptiness. So, we realise we are indestructible in this way and this is ultimately what frees us from all fear and clinging.

Contributors:

RTR: Ringu Tulku Rinpoche
MH: Mary Heneghan
JM: Jonathan Michie
DF: David Fry
FDC: Fiona Duxbury Crosse
YP: Yeshe Palmo

Acknowledgements

Thank you to Jonathan Michie, President of Kellogg College, for inviting Ringu Tulku to give the original talk on which this book is based. It was a joyful and well-attended event which brought together a wide range of people to discuss and contemplate themes central to all our lives. Thank you to the college team who orchestrated the professional, smoothly-run occasion, including Kabi Puliyadi, the event co-ordinator. Thank you to Jonathan also for the inspiring Foreword offered within this book.

Thank you to the organisers of the further talks and teachings drawn on for this book: The White Tara Group in Oxford for the teaching given at Thrangu House in May 2024, on the topic of 'Sangha, the third Jewel;' Bodhicharya Berlin for the teachings given in Berlin in October 2024; Ela Crain for Ringu Tulku's talk on 'Joy and rejoicing' given at Sintra, Portugal, in August 2024; and Humkara Dzong, Portugal, for Ringu Tulku's teachings on The Eightfold Path given in August 2010. Also, thank you to the archivists and custodians of The Ringu Tulku Archive where Ringu Tulku's recorded teachings are held and made easily available for all.

Thank you to Marcy McCall MacBain and the McCall MacBain Foundation for their generous sponsorship towards the publication of this book and for supporting this endeavour in general.

Thank you to John Smythe for his meticulous proof reading and editing advice and ongoing support for the project. Thank you to Ringu Tulku for his unending interest and enthusiasm to meet new people and talk in new places, and for bringing his great wealth of knowledge and wisdom to meet us wherever we are.

Mary Heneghan
for Ocean of Wisdom Publishing

About the Author

Ringu Tulku Rinpoche is a Tibetan Buddhist Master of the Kagyu Order. He was trained in all schools of Tibetan Buddhism under many great masters including His Holiness the 16th Gyalwang Karmapa and His Holiness Dilgo Khyentse Rinpoche. He took his formal education at Namgyal Institute of Tibetology, Sikkim and Sampurnananda Sanskrit University, Varanasi, India. He served as Tibetan Textbook Writer and Professor of Tibetan Studies in Sikkim for 25 years.

Since 1990, he has been travelling and teaching Buddhism and meditation in Europe, America, Canada, Australia and Asia. He participates in various interfaith and 'Science and Buddhism' dialogues and is the author of several books on Buddhist topics. These include *Path to Buddhahood, Daring Steps, The Ri-me Philosophy of Jamgon Kongtrul the Great, Confusion Arises as Wisdom,* the *Lazy Lama* series and the *Heart Wisdom* series, as well as several children's books, available in Tibetan and European languages.

He founded the organisations Bodhicharya and Rigul Trust:

www.bodhicharya.org

www.rigultrust.org.uk

A vast store of his recorded teachings, given over many years and updated weekly, is available in The Ringu Tulku Archive, including video and audio formats:

www.bodhicharya.org/teachings

Mary Heneghan

Mary originally studied Medicine at the University of Oxford, receiving a BA(Hons) MA in Physiological Sciences. She studied Psychology for a further two years at Oxford, completing an MSc by research, in Psychological Disorders. As a medical student, and later as a research assistant, she followed her interests to understand medicine and healing from other cultural perspectives, visiting and working in several African countries and learning from traditional approaches.

She went on to train clinically in acupuncture, and has worked as an acupuncturist since 2000. She now teaches acupuncture, as well as meditation, and kum nye - a meditative, healing yoga from the Tibetan Buddhist tradition. She has written up many of Ringu Tulku's teachings in the form of small books, notably the *Heart Wisdom* series published by Bodhicharya Publications. She is particularly interested in exploring paths of awakening through embodied understanding, and in sharing understanding across cultures.

Ocean of Wisdom Publishing is a non-profit Community Interest Company. All profits go towards writing up and publishing further texts of Buddhist and similar teachings. This project was kindly sponsored by the McCall MacBain Foundation, for which we are indebted. Thank you to Marcy McCall MacBain in particular for her support of this work. May it be of great benefit.

"The Dharma is nobody's property. It belongs to whoever is most interested."
Patrul Rinpoche, 'Words of My Perfect Teacher'

This work is licensed under Creative Commons Licence CC BY-NC-SA 4.0

Creative Commons Attribution-Non-Commercial- ShareAlike 4.0 International

This licence allows re-users to distribute, remix, adapt, and build upon the material in any medium or format, for non-commercial purposes only, and only so long as attribution is given to the creator. If you remix, adapt, or build upon the material, you must license the modified material under identical terms.

- BY: Credit must be given to the creator.

- NC: Only non-commercial use of the work is permitted. Non-commercial means not primarily intended for or directed towards commercial advantage or monetary compensation.

- SA: Adaptations must be shared under the same terms.

For licence details visit:
https://creativecommons.org/licenses/by-nc-sa/4.0/

McCall MacBain Foundation